A SHORT HISTORICAL

AND

ARCHÆOLOGICAL INTRODUCTION

TO

ANCIENT
TRIPOLITANIA

by

D.E.L. HAYNE

CONTENTS

INDEX TO ILLUSTRATIONS

MAPS

FOREWORD

This little book has been written primarily as a guide for the military tourist and makes no claim to original scholarship. It has been prepared in haste and probably contains more than its share of inaccuracy and dogmatic statement; both of which the reader is asked to excuse.

The note on the prehistory of Tripolitania was very kindly written for me by Lieutenant Colonel P. Sandison of the British Military Administration. I have also had the advantage of visiting Leptis and Sabratha with Mr. J.B. Ward Perkins, the first Antiquities Officer of this territory, and I have made wide use of the very valuable information he gave me on those sites. I am greatly indebted to Mr. R.G. Goodchild for reading the proofs and seeing them through the press. Lastly I have been continually helped by Professor Giacomo Caputo and the other members of the staff of the Sopraintendenza ai Monumenti e Scavi della Libia, to all of whom I am glad to have this opportunity of expressing my thanks.

Tripoli, June 1946.

D.E.L.H.

PART I

HISTORICAL SUMMARY

i. A Note on the Prehistory of Tripolitania.

The prehistoric period of human history covers the time from man's emergence up to the invention of writing. Its documents are the implements man made from imperishable materials, his bones and those of the animals he ate, which are often preserved by fossilization, and the engravings and models he made.

The period is generally divided into the Paleolithic, Mesolithic and Neolithic ages. The dating of these periods is still largely a matter of conjecture; but it is fairly certain that a creature distinguishable from the anthropoid apes had emerged in Europe by the time the second glacial period was over. It would not be over-estimating to date this as 125,000 years ago.

In Europe, the amount of research and excavation which has taken place during the last hundred years permits the division of the main periods by reference to the changing fauna associated with human remains and implements. In Africa exploration has not yet produced sufficient evidence. As an example, all the traces of prehistoric man in Tripolitania which have so far been found are stone implements picked up on the present land surface. In Cyrenaica, only one site has been excavated. The dating and correlation of these implements with those found elsewhere is therefore quite conjectural. It can, however, be said that, in all probability the northern shore of Tripolitania in the days of Paleolithic man was roughly along the line of the Homs, Tarhuna, Garian range of hills; and that the climate was much damper. Towards the end of the Paleolithic, it probably grew colder, and man took to living in rock shelters. During the Mesolithic there appears to have been a gradual recession of the sea shore and a dessiccation of the climate, until, in the Neolithic both the coast line and the climate approximated to those of today.

During these three periods there is a gradual evolution in the type of implement made by man. His earliest tools were large stones of which he had sharpened one or more edges by knocking off chips. He then improved his workmanship, and produced an implement almond-shaped, symmetrical and chipped more or less evenly on both faces (the *coup de poing*) (1)*. His next improvement was to chip one face of a piece of stone until it resembled one side of a *coup de poing* and then with a single powerful and well-directed blow strike the shaped portion off the block, thus producing a large flake with one side worked and the other flat. Such an implement, which had a sharp cutting edge all round, is known as a Levallois flake (2).

About this time he seems to have realized the undoubted superiority of flint to other kinds of stone for ease of working and regularity of splitting. And soon flint is in general use. He then found a means of striking long thin blades from a block, or « core » of flint after he had made one end of the block into a « striking platform » or flat surface at right angles

* Figures in brackets refer to folding chart after page 16.

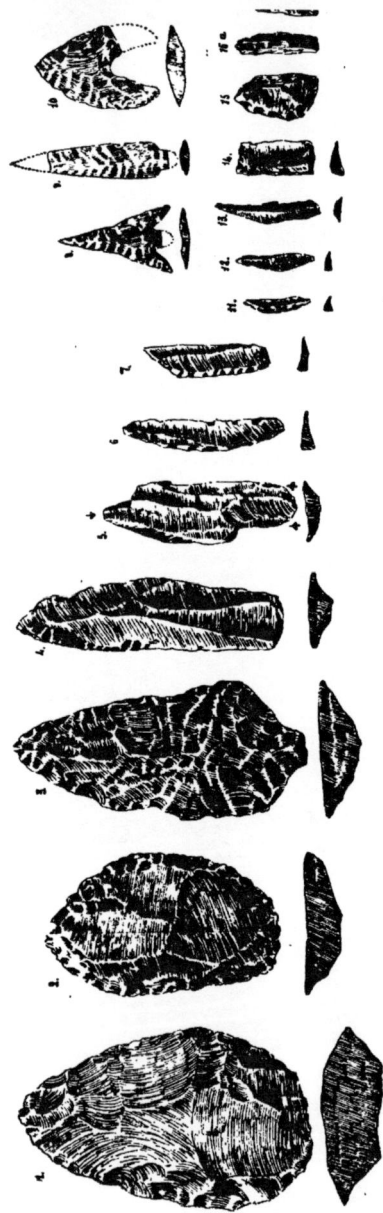

1. Acheulean Hand-axe from Haglet el Tera near Benghazi.

2. Levallois flake from Bocca, S. Tripolitania.

3. Aterian point from Garamas, Fezzan.

4. Capsian blade with retouching from Haglet el Tera.

5. Capsian burin from Haglet el Tera.

6. Large blade from the coastal plain.

7. Backed blade from Haglet el Tera.

8, 9 Neolithic arrowheads from the coastal plain.

10 Concave base arrowhead Fayoum type from Castel Benito.

11, 12, 13. Microlithic backed blades from the coastal plain.

14 Trapezium rectangle, backed on three sides, from the coastal plain.

15a and 15b Three aspects of a microscraper, from the coastal plain.

NOTE The terms in heavy type are employed to give the reader an idea of the balance between social requirements and that of the classical civilizations. Knowledge is not transparent to any scholar or and the majority of the local circumstances were the proper of the classic environment.

to the greatest length of the block (4). Henceforth his progress is rapid. Implements become smaller and less clumsy, and many are designed to be used as spear-heads (3) or barbs. A series of blades carefully blunted on one edge and about the size of the blade of the modern pocket-knife is found (6, 7). Instruments obviously designed for engraving and boring appear (5).

His next discovery is the art of detaching small flakes by pressure instead of percussion. This discovery led to a further improvement in technique; and really beautiful implements of small size and shaped by the removal of tiny flakes all over both faces appear (11-15). His last achievement was the invention of the arrow-head, with or without barbs (8, 9, 10).

In Tripolitania, implements of the *coup de poing* type (1) have as yet been discovered only to the south of the Homs-Garian hills. Levallois flakes (2) and associated types are found both to the south of and in these hills. Flint blades, pressure flaking and arrow heads are found over the whole country, right up to the present coast-line and down to the depths of the Fezzan oases (4-15).

From present evidence it can be said that the Paleolithic man who made the *coups de poing* and the Levallois flakes in Tripolitania, was the same race who dwelt in Egypt and Tunisia. The blade culture, which arose towards the end of the Paleolithic period in Europe, resembles that of Tunisia to which the name of Capsian has been given. Capsian has not yet been found in Egypt, and although Tripolitanian finds resemble Capsian in most respects, the engraving implement, or « burin », which is the principal type instrument of the Capsian has yet to be found.

The Mesolithic cultures of Europe, named Solutrean,

Magdalenian and Tardenoisian, have not been found in North Africa, where we pass directly from the Capsian (Upper Paleolithic) to the Neolithic. It is agreed that the appearance of the arrow-head marks the beginning of the Neolithic. In Tripolitania it seems likely that we have two Neolithic people, a northern and a southern. The southern, found in the Fezzan, resembles that found in the Fayoum in Egypt. The main points of resemblance are rock engravings showing bulls with a round disc, symbolizing the sun, between their horns (Fig. 1), and arrow heads without any tang, known as concave-based (10). In the north, there are objects closely resembling those of the Capsian-type Neolithic (8, 9, 11, 12, 13, 14, 15).

ii. THE LIBYANS.

At the beginning of history the inhabitants of Tripolitania were probably substantially the same peoples as had lived there in Neolithic times. Herodotus, writing in the fifth century B.C., says that Libya (by which he means the whole of North Africa with the exception of Egypt) was inhabited by only two indigenous races: the Libyans and the Aethiopians, of whom the former dwelt in the coastal areas, the latter in the interior. This broad division has been upheld by modern anthropology. Herodotus' « Aethiopians » correspond to the negroid and distinctively African element of the population, to some extent infiltrated into the coastal areas from the Sahara; while his Libyans, from whom the present-day Berbers are descended, were a people of Mediterranean, rather than African, stock who are also found in various parts of southern Europe.

Fig. 1. — Rock Picture (Maia Dib, Fezzan)

Until they came into contact with the Bronze Age culture of the Phœnicians, and in remoter areas probably until much later, the Libyans of Tripolitania were still living in a protracted Neolithic state of development and using stone implements. But this does not necessarily imply great primitiveness. We know that they had already learned to cultivate cereals, as the remains of Neolithic querns show; and in some places they had perhaps formed settled communities living in houses or troglodytic dwellings. Nomadism of a kind there certainly was. Herodotus mentions the Nasamones, a people of eastern Tripolitania, who made an annual migration to the oasis of Augila for the date harvest; and according to another Greek source (fourth century B.C.), the Macae, who inhabited the Homs area, went up into the Jebel every summer to water their cattle. But seasonal movements of this kind, often combined with regular cultivation, cannot be held to be true nomadism, though they may easily be mistaken for such. Moreover, one of the largest of the Tripolitanian tribes, the Garamantes, were certainly sedentary in the Fezzan, where they raised cattle whose peculiarity it was (according to ancient writers, but not according to modern zoologists) to move backwards while grazing owing to the inconvenience of their forward-curving horns. We also learn from Herodotus that this tribe used four-horsed chariots in which they hunted the Aethiopian troglodytes, presumably for slaves; and it is interesting to note that such chariots appear in rock drawings found in the Fezzan (Fig. 2). The Garamantes, who play a large part in the subsequent history of Tripolitania, were generally classified by the ancients as « Aethiopians » (i.e. negroid), but the results of an Italian archaeological and anthropological expedition to the Fezzan, during which some 45,000 of their tombs were found in the Wadi el-Agial, suggest that they were in fact of Mediterranean stock.

Of the social life of the Libyans we know very little. Customs seem to have varied from tribe to tribe; but there was a common language and certain religious beliefs were widely shared. To judge from rock engravings, animal totemism formed an important element of the latter; and pictures of a bull with a solar disc between its horns (to be identified with the Egyptian god Ammon-Râ), of which mention has already been made above (p. 17 and fig. 1), point to a widespread

Fig. 2. — Rock Picture. (Wadi Zigza, Fezzan)

cult of the sun, which is also attested by Herodotus.
With the worship of the sun Herodotus couples worship
of the moon, but this was perhaps a Phœnician impor-
tation and not indigenous. In spite of linguistic and
religious uniformity, only once in their history (it was
during the period of the Numidian kingdom) did the

Libyans achieve any large measure of political unity, the development of which was normally hindered by their division into numerous tribes and their intolerance of any form of centralized authority. In a sense it may be said that their love of autonomy was carried so far as to be self-defeating, for *divide et impera* was the policy with which their successive masters were able to hold them down during the greater part of ancient history. Nevertheless they never resigned themselves to the loss of their freedom; and their tenacious attempts to regain it are not the least significant events of Tripolitanian history.

iii. THE PHŒNICIAN COLONIZATION.

Near the end of the second millennium B.C. the Tripolitanian coast began to be visited by Phœnician sailors from the thriving ports of Tyre and Sidon in Syria. The Phœnicians were a people of great commercial enterprise who ranged far and wide along the shores of the Mediterranean, and even beyond the Straits of Gibraltar, in search of gold, silver and other rarities which could be bought cheaply from the naive barbarians of the west and sold expensively in the sophisticated markets of the east. They were the middlemen and traders of the ancient world, to whom even Solomon had recourse when every three years he sent his ships, manned by Phœnicians « that had knowledge of the sea, » to bring back « gold and silver, ivory and apes and peacocks » from the west.

In was necessity, however, more probably than enterprise, which first induced the Phœnicians to set foot in such an apparently unpromising land as Tripolitania. Sea voyages in the little ships of those times were perilous undertakings; and ancient sailors played for safety by following the coast-line to their destination rather than cross the open sea. In the course of their voyages to and from the more lucrative western end of the Mediterranean the Phœnicians must often have passed along the Tripolitanian coast; and from time to time, no doubt, the treacherous storms and calms of the Sirtic gulf drove them to put in there for shelter or fresh supplies. Thus fairly early certain recognized calling places may have been established along the coast where ships could be sure of finding a safe anchorage and native agents ready to satisfy their needs.

It cannot have been long, however, before these casual contacts opened the Phœnicians' eyes to the possibility of deriving more than transitory advantages from their visits to Tripolitania. Although the coastal plain had little to offer on its own account, it was the terminus of some of the easiest and shortest routes linking the Mediterranean with the African interior where gold, ivory, ostrich-plumes, slaves and other valuable commodities were to be found in plenty. This was an opportunity of which the Phœnicians would not have been slow to avail themselves; and though for a time they may have been content with developing the more suitably situated of their calling stations into native markets without themselves settling there, they soon began to think in the more ambitious terms of colonization.

The date of the Phœnician colonization of Tripolitania has been much debated, some authorities placing it as early as the twelfth century B.C. others as late as the eighth. There are no good reasons for going to either extreme and it seems preferable to think of it as a gradual process lasting perhaps for the first two centuries of the first millennium B.C. This was a period during which many of the other Phœnician colonies in the west were founded, including Carthage; and it may well have been a time of political and social unrest in Tyre and Sidon, the consequence of the Assyrian aggression of the period.

Place names recorded by Greek geographers suggest that the Phœnicians settled at as many as ten points along the Tripolitanian coast, but most of their settlements can have been little more than outposts with a small minority of Phœnician traders among the native population. Of such lesser places Carax, perhaps to be identified with Medinet-es-Sultan between Sirte and Nofilia, later became noted for a contraband trade in Cyrenaic silphium and Tripolitanian wine; Sirte itself, which was known as Euphrantas Tower, had a good harbour which the Phœnicians used; while Macomaca in the Tauorga lagoon and Zouchis (or Zeucharis) a day's sailing to the west of Tripoli achieved some importance by their fish-preserving industries. Zouchis was also known for its purple dyes derived from the cuttle-fish by a process for which the Phœnicians were famous throughout antiquity.

It was only at three places that the Phœnicians established true colonies, transforming the original trading stations into Phœnician towns and settling there in large numbers. The places they chose possessed various advantages. Leptis or Lepcis—the original form of the name, *Lpqy*, suggests a pre-existing Libyan settlement—lay in one of the most fertile areas of Tripolitania. The proximity of the hills to the sea caused a relatively heavy rainfall; and a perennial stream, the

Wadi Caam, watered the plain to the east of the town. The town itself was built at the mouth of the Wadi Lebda which afforded a good anchorage for ships under the protection of an out-lying reef on the west. The second colony, which the Phœnicians called Uai'at and the Greeks and Romans Oea, was founded where Tripoli now stands. Here too the combination of a wadi mouth (Wadi Mejenin) and a projecting line of reef provided a roadstead. The extensive oases by which the colony was surrounded, furnished ample food and water to support it; and it was well placed to monopolize the trade coming from the interior by way of the Tarhuna and Garian gaps. Finally, Sabratha, which still preserves the Phœnician form of its name fairly closely, was established at the head of an important trade route leading up to the coast through Gadames. But for this commanding position the colonists paid in other ways, for Sabratha had no natural harbour; only a line of reefs running parallel to the coast sheltered it from the force of the open sea. Nor was the surrounding countryside particularly fertile or well supplied with water, the provision of which must always have been a problem for the Sabrathans.

iv. THE CARTHAGINIAN DOMINATION.

Little is known of the earliest history of the three colonies or Libyan Emporia as they came to be called from the Greek word *emporion* meaning a commercial centre. Any imperial ties which may have subordinated them to their mother-country at the beginning must soon have been relaxed, for Tyre, the capital of Phœnicia, was finally subjected to the Assyrians by the end of the eighth century B.C., and thereafter the only bounds between Phœnicia and the western colonies were purely cultural and religious ones. Meanwhile a new Phœnician power was rising in the west to take the place of Tyre and lead the western colonies in their struggle against the expanding maritime power of Greece by which they now began to be seriously threatened. Carthage, a Tyrian colony founded at the end of the ninth century B.C. close to the site of modern Tunis, was well fitted by her power and geographical position to assume the leadership of the Phœnicians; and there can be little doubt that had she not united the colonies, they would have perished singly. But the price of her protection was a heavy one. The colonies were compelled to surrender their independence to the dominant partner, and what might have been a voluntary confederation was soon transformed into a Carthaginian empire.

There is no record of the date of the incorporation of the Emporia in the Carthaginian Empire, but an episode which happened towards the end of the sixth century suggests that it may have been finally accomplished then. In 520 B.C. Dorieus, son of the Spartan king Anaxandridas, having quarrelled with his brother who had succeeded to the throne, decided to leave his native land taking with him a number of Spartans who were willing to share his project. Guided by inhabitants of the Greek island of Thera—whose kinsfolk had already colonized Cyrenaica and must have looked with favour on a westward extension of Greek power in North Africa—Dorieus disembarked in Tripolitania at the mouth of the Wadi Caam (the ancient Cinyps) where he founded a colony. But the venture was short-lived for three years later the Carthaginians, with the help of a local Libyan tribe called the Macæ, drove the colonists into the sea.

Such is the story as Herodotus tells it, but it is not easy to see why Carthage's reaction should have been so slow, or why there is no mention of Leptis having taken part in the colony's destruction, though she lay barely twelve miles to the west of it and could not have regarded with indifference the alien occupation of some of her most fertile territory. None of the explanations so far given is entirely satisfactory; but it is arguable that Leptis may still have been outside the sphere of Carthaginian protection when Dorieus came, and feeling herself too weak to oppose the Greeks single-handed may have preferred to come to terms with them. The Carthaginians themselves cannot have attached much importance to the Greek colony at first: otherwise they would scarcely have allowed Dorieus three years' grace in which to consolidate his position. It was probably its later rapid development which awoke them to the potential danger of a Greek foothold in Tripolitania and convinced them of the necessity not only of expelling Dorieus, but of including Leptis and the other Emporia in their empire. At all events from 517 B.C. onwards the Emporia were no longer independent cities.

The extension of their empire into Tripolitania brought the Carthaginians into contact and conflict with the powerful Greek colony of Cyrene, already fast becoming one of the foremost cities of the Greek world; but the historical evidence for the war between the two powers is so embedded in a later legend that it is difficult to distinguish fiction from fact. The Cyreneans and the Carthaginians, according to the legend, had long been engaged in heavy and interminable warfare by land

and sea because of the impossibility of establishing a clearly defined frontier in the featureless desert which lay between them. Weary at length of fighting and fearful lest their increasing weakness might invite aggression by a third party, both sides agreed to the simultaneous despatch of envoys from Cyrene and Carthage to settle the frontier at the point where they met. The Carthaginians sent two brothers called the Philainoi who made excellent speed, but the Cyrenean representatives dawdled or were delayed and had only covered a third of the distance achieved by their rivals when the meeting occurred. Alarmed by the probable consequences of this sluggardly exhibition when it became known at home, the Cyreneans confused the issue by accusing the Carthaginians of having cheated. The Carthaginians then invited the Greeks to propose a further test, provided that it should be equal for both parties; and the Greeks suggested that the Philainoi should either allow themselves to be buried alive at the spot where they (the Philainoi) wished to draw the frontier, or should allow the Greeks to advance to the point where they (the Greeks) would be willing to draw it on the same conditions. The Philainoi accepted the challenge and were buried alive where they stood, the place of their sacrifice being later commemorated by the erection of two funeral mounds known as the altars of the Philainoi.

The many absurdities in this story cast suspicion on such elements of truth as it may contain. Certainly the frontier between Tripolitania and Cyrenaica was marked by two mounds by the middle of the fourth century B.C., since the mounds are mentioned in a Greek geographical work of this date. But they are there called simply the mounds of Philainos, Philainos being the name of a village near which they were built. In Greek however, the word Philainos bears the meaning *lover of fame*; and it was no doubt this double meaning, together with the similarity of the two mounds to tombs, which gave rise to the tale of the fame-loving brothers and their patriotic death. Probably the only historical facts are the preliminary war and the final establishment of an agreed frontier. Even the « heavy and interminable warfare » appears an exaggeration. Given the nature of the country in which it was fought, it can hardly have amounted to more than intermittent guerrilla operations. The date of the whole episode is wrapped in characteristic legendary vagueness, but since the mounds of Philainos were already established by the middle of the fourth century B.C., the settlement they marked may perhaps be placed in the later fifth. The place where the mounds are believed to have stood is now marked by Mussolini's Marble Arch.

The settlement thus reached remained in force until near the end of the fourth century B.C. and Tripolitania during this period seems to have enjoyed a peaceful, if obscure, existence under Carthaginian rule. But the unaggressive policy which Cyrene followed so long as she was a free city, was reversed by her Macedonian conquerors. Alexander himself was prevented by his death in 323 B.C. from carrying out his threat of marching against Carthage by way of Tripolitania, for which his proclamation as the son of the Libyan god Jove Ammon at the oasis of Siwa had seemed such ominous propaganda. But the heir of his Egyptian conquests, Ptolemy I Soter. having made good his claim to Cyrenaica by force of arms, carried its western boundary forward to Sirte, 200 miles beyond the mounds of Philainos. Carthage's reaction to this operation is not recorded. She was in any case heavily engaged with the

Sicilian Greeks at the time and may not have been in a position to take any immediate action in Tripolitania. But an unforeseen development in the Sicilian war now brought the threat of the Cyrenean Greeks home to her and caused much incidental damage in Tripolitania.

In 410 B.C. Agathocles, the tyrant of Syracuse (on which city the leadership of the Sicilian Greeks had by now devolved) unexpectedly decided to carry the war into the enemy's camp by landing in Tunisia, where he quickly achieved some remarkable successes. But finding himself insufficiently strong to force a final decision, he called on Ophellas, the Macedonian governor of Cyrene, for aid, promising him a free hand in Libya in the event of success. Ophellas, an ambitious and independent adventurer, readily agreed to an offer which probably precipitated designs of his own. Collecting an army of 10,000 infantry, 600 cavalry and 100 chariots, together with a baggage column of some 10,000 men, women and children, he set out in the summer of 309 or 308 B.C. to join his Syracusan ally. It was a slow and painful journey along the barren coast of the Sirtic gulf. The heat of the season and the lack of food and water inflicted terrible suffering on a host which was said to have resembled a whole colony on the march rather than a disciplined army. For days together lotus-fruit was their only fare; and many died of hunger, thirst and snake-bites. History is silent on the fate of the Emporia at the hands of this famished and desperate multitude, but there can be little doubt that they fell upon the countryside like locusts, devouring everything that lay in their path. The Emporia, with no armies of their own and no prospect of help from hard-pressed Carthage, can have done little to stop them. But the visitation passed; and two and a half months after leaving Cyrene Ophellas joined forces with Agathocles in Tunisia.

The meeting did neither of them any good. Shortly after his arrival Agathocles treacherously contrived to have Ophellas murdered; but even with the addition of Ophellas' troops to his own the decisive victory still eluded him and he was at length compelled to return to Sicily unsuccessful. Carthage, on the other hand, quickly recovered from her temporary setbacks. Not only did she reassert her authority as far as the mounds of Philainos without, it seems, encountering any serious opposition from Magias, an illegitimate son of Ptolemy who had succeeded Ophellas at Cyrene, but she also returned to her Sicilian intrigues with such good effect that by the middle of the third century B.C. she controlled virtually the whole island with the exception of Syracuse. The Carthaginian empire now stood at the height of its power and on the edge of disaster. It is perhaps a convenient moment to consider briefly the effects of Carthaginian domination on the internal affairs of the Emporia.

The over riding interests of Carthage in the Emporia were commercial and strategic. So long as their trade and foreign relations remained under her control, she was probably indifferent to their domestic affairs in which they were allowed a great measure of freedom. Their constitutions, like her own, were inherited from the Phœnician cities by which they were founded and she had no reason to wish to alter them. At Leptis—and the same may safely be inferred for Oea and Sabratha —a popular assembly annually elected two magistrates called Sufetes, who were responsible for the city's civil administration in which they were assisted by a small council formed from the ranks of the most prominent citizens. Since the influence and authority of this council far outweighed that of the popular assembly, the government was in effect narrowly oligarchial, and no doubt reflected the interests of the ruling class—and Carthage—very faithfully. The Sufetes also possessed supreme judicial and military authority; but the latter can only have been a formality, for the Emporia were not permitted to maintain armies or war-fleets. Their defence was undertaken by Carthage who demanded in return contingents of recruits and payment in money and foodstuffs.

The benefits of internal autonomy were, however, largely offset by the rigid and jealous control which Carthage exercised over the foreign relations of the Emporia. By treaty or by force she had already closed their harbours to the shipping of other nations by the end of the sixth century B.C. and the episode of Dorieus shows how little disposed she was to tolerate foreign competition in her own preserves. Deprived of any other outlet for their trade the Emporia were forced to sell to Carthage at her own price; and since Carthage's own port remained open to all comers, it soon developed a thriving monopoly at the expense of her dependencies. The depressing effect of such a policy on the Emporia is not difficult to imagine; it reduced them to a condition of economic slavery and left them in a cultural backwater. And in the outcome it did more harm than good to Carthage herself. When later she was in desperate straits in her struggle with Rome, the Emporia had neither the means nor the inclination to come to her aid.

Denied the income of a profitable foreign trade, the Emporia must have depended to a great extent on

agriculture for their economic well-being. The Phœnicians were among the most skilful agriculturalists of
antiquity and Carthaginian farming treatises were well
known to the Greeks and Romans. In Tripolitania the
Libyans had grown cereals since early times; but the
Phœnicians brought with them scientific methods and
improved implements; and it is very likely that they
initiated some of the irrigation systems which were later
so extensively developed by the Romans. The results
were impressive to judge from the enthusiastic, though
clearly exaggerated, account given by Herodotus of the
crops in the Wadi Caam area which, he says, produced
a yield of 300 for 1 and were equal to those of Babylon.
But the most valuable contribution made by the Phœnicians to Tripolitanian agriculture was undoubtedly the
introduction of scientific fruit-tree farming, for which the
country's climate with its long periods of drought and
its scorching winds is much better adapted than for
cereal growing. Probably the only fruit-tree cultivated
in Tripolitania before the Phœnicians came, was the
date palm, a tree which can only grow in a relatively
damp soil. The Phœnicians developed many less exacting varieties, such as the almond, fig, peach and
pomegranate; and, above all, the vine and olive which
were to become the mainstay of Tripolitania's internal
economy.

About other aspects of the life of the Emporia little
is known. Archæological discoveries have been too few
and too sporadic to enable a coherent picture to be
formed. Among religious cults that of Tanit (the
Heavenly Queen) seems to have been the most widespread, but Baal Ammon (God of the Sky), Echmun
(God of Healing), and Melqart (the Phœnician Hercules) were also worshipped. The arts appear to have been

but poorly developed if the crude pottery vessels found in Phœnician tombs are fair specimens of the standard generally attained. The Phœnicians, however, were never a people of much originality or creative ability. Side by side with local pottery Greek vases are found which were probably imported from South Italy by way of Carthage; they are an interesting tribute to the prestige of Greek art in an obscure Phœnician colony, but little more; for they seldom rise above the level of mass-produced export ware.

v. THE NUMIDIAN KINGDOM.

By the middle of the third century B.C., the Romans had supplanted the Greeks as the most powerful European people in the Mediterranean. While she was still consolidating her position in Italy Rome had been content to allow her commercial interests in North Africa to be limited by treaties between herself and Carthage; but now that she had become a first-class power, and the Carthaginian threat had reached the threshold of Italy with the occupation of Messina, the time for counter-measures had arrived. In the First Punic War (264-241 B.C.) she threw the Carthaginians out of Sicily, but left their African empire untouched. Carthage soon recovered and returned to the fight in the Second Punic War (218-202 B.C.), in which Hannibal's brilliant campaign in Italy all but gave her the victory. But crossing into Africa Scipio Africanus won a decisive battle near Zama in Tunisia and the Carthaginians asked for terms. It would have been logical perhaps, and certainly less disastrous for Carthage in the outcome, if she had now passed into the immediate control of Rome. The Romans, however, were not yet prepared to assume any direct commitment in Africa themselves, but hoped to be able to keep Carthage in subjection by indirect means. They had been helped during the war by a Numidian chief, Masinissa, under whom a number of discontented tribes revolted against Carthage after proclaiming the formation of an independent Numidian kingdom. This kingdom Rome now officially recognized and entered into an alliance with Masinissa, partly as a reward for his services, but principally because she saw in him a zealous policeman who would effectively check any future Carthaginian aspirations with the minimum of trouble to herself. Carthage herself lost her fleet (it was reduced to the innocuous total of ten triremes) and was compelled to cede to Masinissa a large area of her richest territory which he claimed as rightfully belonging to the Numidian kingdom. The Emporia, however, to which Masinissa could show no legal title, were left in Carthage's possession.

But Masinissa was not a person to be restrained by legal scruples for long when a prize as attractive and apparently as easy as the Emporia presented itself. On the pretext of pursuing a rebel who had escaped to Cyrenaica, he asked Carthage for permission to march through Tripolitania, which Carthage, rightly suspecting his intentions, refused. Masinissa then threw aside pretences and marched against the Emporia openly, but his attempts to take them were frustrated by the efforts of the citizens themselves who, though they had no love for Carthage, had even less for a barbarian upstart and defiantly shut themselves within their walls. Carthage, meanwhile, appealed to Rome against the flagrant infringement of the peace-treaty; and the Romans, caught in a dilemma between condoning the infrigement or offending a useful ally, temporized for a while by sending commissions of inquiry to Africa. But eventually in 162 B.C. the Senate ordered Carthage to surrender the Emporia, though it appears that it was not until about 150 that Masinissa finally gained control over them.

In 148 Masinissa died and two years later Carthage, whose reviving agriculture had once more aroused the jealousy of the influential land-owning class of Rome, was razed to the ground as the result of the short Third Punic War. Neither of these events can have caused much regret in the Emporia; but if they hoped that as the result of them they would be liberated from Numidian rule and incorporated in the Roman empire (which must already have begun to appear a desirable end), they were disappointed; although the Romans formed an African province from Carthage's territory, they continued to recognize an independent Numidian kingdom under Masinissa's successors to whom the Emporia were still subject. Apart, however, from the necessity of paying taxes, the Emporia seem to have been left very much to their own devices. The Numidian government was too distant and too inefficient to do much to interfere in their every-day life, however much it might hurt their pride. Meanwhile they cultivated good relations with Rome; and when in 111 B.C. Jugurtha, a pretender to the Numidian throne, involved the kingdom in a civil war in which the Romans were obliged to intervene, Leptis (and probably Oea and Sabratha) applied to Rome for a treaty of friendship and alliance which was readily granted. A little later Leptis asked for a Roman garrison to defend her against a threatened rebel plot within her own walls; and for the first time

Roman troops were stationed in Tripolitania. From now onwards Roman influence in the Emporia increased rapidly and Roman merchants probably settled there in increasing numbers; but it was not until the time of Cæsar that they were finally incorporated in the Roman empire.

vi. THE EARLY IMPERIAL PERIOD.

During the civil war between Cæsar and Pompey, the King of Numidia, Juba I, a personal enemy of Cæsar, had declared for the Pompeians and helped them to gain control of the province of Africa. By his victory at Thapsus (46 B.C.), therefore, in which both the Pompeians and the Numidians were finally defeated, Cæsar gained a free hand to dispose of both the province and the kingdom as he wished. The province was retained with its former boundaries; but the kingdom, (whose independent existence under unruly princelings had done more harm than good to Rome) was abolished, and the greater part of its territory, including Tripolitania, constituted the new province of Africa Nova, the original province now being called Africa Vetus. Although there is evidence ([1]) to suggest that Leptis supported the Pompeians in the civil war and was compelled to pay Cæsar a heavy indemnity in olive oil after his victory, the Emporia must have been well satisfied with his settlement which offered them a prospect of

(1)   Some doubt exists here (as on some other occasions) as to whether the Leptis referred to in the sources is the Tripolitanian one, or a smaller Leptis in Tunisia, from which the Tripolitanian city is usually distinguished by being called Leptis Magna.

peace and commercial prosperity under Roman protection. Nor were they directly affected by the civil war which followed the murder of Cæsar in 44 B.C., though they must have followed its developments in Africa with anxiety until the final triumph of Augustus in 25 B.C. assured them that the advantages they had so lately won were not to be taken from them.

With the return of peace within the empire the legions which had spent the last fifty years or more fighting one another, were free to fight the enemies of Rome along her frontiers. To Africa, which now became a single province by the fusion of Africa Vetus and Africa Nova, Augustus sent the Legio III Augusta which set up its headquarters at Theveste in Tunisia and stationed detachments at strategic points throughout the province including the territory of the Emporia. Contrary to his usual practice of retaining personal control of frontier provinces where the presence of troops was necessary, Augustus assigned the government of Africa to the Senate who administered it through a proconsul; and until the reign of Caligula (A.D. 37-41), the proconsul also commanded the legion. The province was divided into dioceses each administered by a proconsular legate; but it is not certain whether Tripolitania formed an independent diocese by itself, or whether it formed part of another.

Protected by a Roman legion and guided by a liberal and peaceful administration the material prosperity of the Emporia steadily increased. The doors which the Carthaginians had kept so tightly closed were now thrown open to the world. Trade began to flow into the harbours of the Emporia again and wealth into the pockets of their citizens. The old Phœnician towns were transformed into fashionable Roman cities with temples, theatres, market-places and dwelling houses built to Roman designs; comfortable villas and farms spread over the countryside; and Roman methods of irrigation and water conservation brought new life to agriculture.

Though Roman ways of life and thought penetrated the Emporia with remarkable speed and thoroughness, they were not forcibly imposed on the Phœnicians. The Emporia were treated as autonomous allies rather than subject and tributary cities, and the alliance concluded in 111 B.C. was probably still maintained in force. Until the reign of Tiberius (A.D. 14-37) they continued to mint their own coins; and even when this privilege had been withdrawn they retained their old Phœnician magistrates, the Sufetes, and also probably the council and popular assembly of their old constitutions. Bilingual inscriptions show that for some time Phœnician held an equal place with Latin as an official written language; and as a spoken language it survived until the Arab conquest. In religion, too, the introduction of Roman and imperial elements did not abruptly break the Phœnician tradition. The old Phœnician deities were identified with Roman ones: Baal Ammon, for example, with Saturn, Tanit with Juno and Melqart with Hercules; and side by side with them other specifically Roman cults of the emperor and his family in which the provincials' gratitude and loyalty to Rome were expressed.

vii. REVOLTS AND EXPEDITIONS.

While the citizens of the Emporia were reaping the fruits of their new security, the responsibility of defending them fell on the Romans. The foothold of civilization in Tripolitania was still a narrow one. The territories controlled by the Emporia were confined to the coastal area, while the whole unknown interior of the country was in the hands of untamed and warlike peoples ready to take up arms on the slightest pretext. Moreover tension was rapidly increasing as a result of the suppression of the Numidian kingdom in which the natives had seen the symbol of their independence. Between the coastal cities and the interior no readily defensible line existed, and it was, therefore, only by extending their authority far to the south that the Romans could hope to maintain the frontier of civilization intact.

During the early imperial period the greatest danger came from the Garamantes of the Fezzan. At the beginning of Augustus' reign this powerful and unruly tribe rose in sympathy with a revolt which started in Numidia and soon threatened the whole southern frontier of the province. In this crisis Cornelius Balbus, to whom a special command was given to deal with the revolt, decided to direct his main effort against the Fezzan. Setting out in 20 B.C., probably from Sabratha, he marched to Cydamus (Gadames), an important caravan station of the Garamantes, which submitted and appears to have been an « allied city » of Rome from now on. From Cydamus Balbus moved southeast into the Fezzan itself where he captured a number of towns and finally Garama (Germa), the Garamantic capital. After this disaster the rebels gave up the struggle and Balbus returned to celebrate an elaborate triumph at Rome.

But the Garamantes were still far from being completely pacified. Under Tiberius they joined a new and still more serious revolt of the Numidian tribes led by a deserter from the Roman army, Tacfarinas. To suppress this revolt the Legio III Augusta was reinforced by the Legio IX Hispana, and for a time Spanish legionaries were stationed at Leptis to defend the city's territory (part of which, it seems, the Garamantes had been able to seize) and to intercept the rebels, should they attempt to escape from Tunisia—where the revolt was centred—through the territory of the Emporia to the Fezzan. No serious fighting, however, seems to have developed in Tripolitania itself; and when after eight years of guerrilla fighting the revolt came to an end with the defeat and death of Tacfarinas (A.D. 24), the Garamantes sent an embassy to Rome to seek the emperor's pardon.

They might possibly now have resigned themselves to a more peaceful existence, had not the irresponsible behaviour of the Emporia themselves invited them to take up arms once more. In A.D. 69 an apparently trivial border incident in which citizens of Leptis and Oea were involved, developed into a war between the two cities already no doubt divided by long-standing rivalries; and Oea, seeing herself outnumbered, called on the Garamantes for aid. The tribesmen fell on Leptis with a will, devastating the countryside and even laying seige to the city itself, which was, however, saved by its walls. In this plight the citizens of Leptis appealed to the proconsul: and Valerius Festus who came to their rescue, soon succeeded in driving the rebels off to the south. What punishment, if any, he inflicted on Oea for her disastrous alliance, is not recorded; but it is difficult to believe that she can have escaped altogether, though the fact that two of the Emporia were able to make war on one another, shows that they still possessed surprising freedom of action. Festus, however, was mainly concerned with the punishment of the Garamantes, against whose home territory he now decided to march. No details of this second expedition to the Fezzan have survived, except that it started from Leptis and discovered a route four days shorter than that taken by Balbus; it was probably the eastern caravan route leading through Bu Ngem and Hon. Festus' expedition seems to have been entirely successful, for when the Garamantes are next heard of it is as the allies of the Romans in two remarkable expeditions which they undertook from the Fezzan into Central Africa.

The first expedition, led by Septimius Flaccus, made the Fezzan its base for a march of three months into « the midst of the Aethiopians ». The second, under Julius Maternus, set out from Leptis and « having joined the king of the Garamantes at Garama, marched southwards with him against the Aethiopians, arriving after four months' marching at Agysimba where the rhinoceros is found ». Unfortunately these interesting expeditions have come down to us in a single and very summary account which has been suspected of exagger- ating the times involved and which gives no indication of the motives for which they were undertaken. The « Aethiopians » cannot be certainly identified since the ancients gave this name to all the negroid inhabitants of Africa; nor is it possible to locate Agysimba, though Lake Chad has been suggested. But in spite of these uncertainties it is clear that the expeditions were remarkable undertakings with the equipment and geo- graphical knowledge available to the Romans; and it is unlikely that any comparable penetration of the African continent occurred again before the nineteenth century. The expeditions are probably to be dated in the late first or early second century.

Only one other native tribe seriously disturbed the peace of Tripolitania in the early imperial period. In the reign of Domitian (A.D. 81-96) the Nasamones who seem to have been a nomadic people living in eastern Tripolitania, rose in revolt after putting to death some officials sent to collect their taxes. A punitive expedition led by Suellius Flaccus, the commander of the Legio III Augusta, was badly defeated in its first battle and the Roman camp fell into the enemy's hands. But its capture was their undoing. Instead of pursuing the Romans they made merry with the large stock of food and wine they found there; and when the Romans. hearing of their incapable condition, unexpectedly returned to renew the battle, the rebels were easily defeated and routed. Thereafter the Nasamones appear to have lived in peace and to have paid their taxes promptly. ✓ ₁₄\b

viii. THE AGE OF PROSPERITY AND THE DYNASTY OF THE SEVERI.

By the end of the first century the pacification of Tripolitania was complete and Roman authority extended from the Mediterranean to the Fezzan. For the next hundred years, the most peaceful in the history of the western world, the Emporia basked in the « endless summer afternoon of the Roman empire » without the record of a single military event. The caravan routes by which the wealth of the African interior reached the coast, were secure from interruption; and in Rome the

Emporia found a ready market for luxury goods of every kind and especially for the wild and exotic animals which were required in ever increasing numbers for the amphitheatre. The volume of trade was in fact such that both Leptis and Sabratha kept permanent representatives at the Roman port of Ostia. Meanwhile agriculture, relieved of the threat of sudden devastation, was also finding a market in Rome. During the early imperial period the Romans had tended to discourage provincial cultivation of olives in order to favour Italian growers. But now that the impoverishment of Italian soil had begun seriously to threaten even the home supply, they were obliged to reverse this policy and begin importing themselves. For Tripolitania this meant an outlet for the one product she could produce economically and abundantly: and there can be little doubt that she made the most of her opportunity.

It was perhaps the increasing economic importance of the three cities which won for them a greater measure of imperial recognition in the second century; Leptis was raised to the status of a Roman colony under Trajan (A.D. 98-117: *Colonia Ulpia Traiana*), while the other two had been similarly promoted before the end of the century. From now on their citizens enjoyed all the rights and privileges of citizens of Rome. But the most certain proofs of the prosperity of the period may be seen in contemporary monuments. The Great Baths of Leptis, perhaps the most splendid in any provincial city, were dedicated in A.D. 127 under Hadrian. The theatre of Sabratha and probably the whole quarter of the city in which it stands were built in the second century. And though most of Oea has long since vanished under Tripoli, it is perhaps significant that the one monument which has survived more or less intact—the triumphal arch in the Old City—was erected in honour of Marcus Aurelius.

Something of the flavour of intellectual life in the Emporia at this period may be derived from an incident in which the leading part was played by Apuleius of Madaura, a philosopher, orator and author, best known for his fantasy *The Golden Ass*. Apuleius fell ill while on a visit to Oea and wiled away his convalescence by giving public lectures with which the Oeans were so delighted that they invited him to become a citizen and settle in the country. To this Apuleius agreed and shortly after married a wealthy widow of the place, Emilia Pudentilla. But it was the end of his popularity. The widow's relatives, disappointed in their hopes of inheritance, started a whispering campaign against him which culminated in a formal accusation of magical practices. The case was heard at Sabratha before the proconsul Claudius Maximus, himself a philosopher; and Apuleius had no difficulty in rebutting the charge and ridiculing his opponents in a brilliant speech which still survives (*The Apology*). But Tripolitania lost her first and only distinguished man of letters, for Apuleius returned to his own country in disgust.

The end of the Antonine dynasty in A.D. 192 once more plunged the empire into a civil war of accession from which it emerged five years later with a native of Leptis at its head. Born in 146 Septimius Severus came of a well-to-do provincial family which still spoke Phœn-ician at home, though some of its members had already achieved high distinction in Rome as officials of the im-perial government. Septimius followed in their foot-steps. He had already risen to be the commander-in-chief of the Illyrian legions in Pannonia when the dyn-astic confusion of A.D. 193 threw the imperial succession open to any candidate who could support his claim with sufficient military strength to defeat his rivals. Septimius seized an opportunity for which he was probably not unprepared; had himself acclaimed emperor by his own legions; and set about the task of removing his competitors which was to occupy the first four years of his reign.

The civil war did not have any direct repercussions in Tripolitania; but while it was still in progress a Tripolitanian or neighbouring tribe, taking advantage of the general confusion of the empire, ended more than a century of peace by rebelling. Nothing is known of the revolt itself, but it had an important consequence; for having suppressed the rebels Septimius Severus decided to secure his native land against any more such intrusions by reorganizing its defences. Until now the Romans had relied for the defence of Tripolitania on their power to strike deep into the interior and eliminate the danger at its root. The only fixed fortifications probably consisted of more or less disconnected outposts placed along the general line of the Jebel watershed and overlooking the routes leading up to the coast. These disconnected outposts were now linked together by a strategic road running along the top of the Jebel in a great arc from Leptis to Tacape (Gabes) in Tunisia; the outposts themselves were probably strengthened and perhaps increased in number; and the whole defensive system, to which the name *Limes Tripolitanus* or Tripolitanian frontier was given (perhaps the earliest official use of this Greek collective name for the three Emporia), was manned by special troops. « Very brave soldiers from the Tripolitanian frontier » are mentioned in an inscription of A.D. 263. In addition to the *Limes* a number of large independent forts were built at strategic points in the interior of the country, such as Bu Ngem, where routes converged at watering places and could thus be effectively controlled. Septimius' defensive scheme was completed under his successors Caracalla (A.D. 211-217) and Alexander Severus (222-235), from whose reigns some of the existing fortifications date. Alexander further strengthened the defence of the outlying regions by encouraging veteran legionaries (probably Romanized Libyans for the most part) to settle there as soldier-farmers responsible for their own defence in return for a free grant of land, animals and slaves, and exemption from all taxation.

Amid the cares of empire Septimius found time to remember his own birthplace. Leptis, which had long since achieved a leading position among the three Emporia, was now granted the *ius italicum* which carried with it exemption from all taxation of land. The grateful citizens voted an annual gift of olive oil to be distributed free among the poor of Rome (which afterwards became a great burden to the city when later emperors exacted what had at first been voluntarily offered); and it was perhaps on this same occasion that they set up a tablet in the Great Baths commemorating the « exceptional kindness » shown to the « Septimians », as they call themselves, by their emperor. But the good fortune of giving birth to an emperor is most clearly reflected in the splendour and scale of the public buildings with which Leptis was embellished during the reign of Septimius. The Severan forum and basilica form an architectural complex without parallel in the western provinces; and the monumental harbour with its lighthouse is no less impressive in its own way. Apart from these two major works many other important constructions must be ascribed to the Severan period, including

the great nymphæum, the street of columns and probably the southernmost of the two large reservoirs in
the Wadi Lebda outside the city. It is a remarkable
achievement for what was still fundamentally a provincial town of no great importance in the Roman empire;
and a remarkable testimony to the wise provincial government of «the ablest Emperour almost of all the liste».

ix. THE DECLINE.

But the light which shone so radiantly on Tripolitania at the opening of the third century came from
a setting sun. Only a third of the century had passed
when the murder of Alexander Severus brought to an
end the dynasty of her protectors and left the Roman
world a prey to civil wars and barbarian invasions from
which it had neither the spiritual nor the material
strength to recover. The reforms of Diocletian (A.D.
284-305) and Constantine (306-337) could only arrest
this process of disintegration without curing its causes;
and it was of little ultimate profit to Tripolitania that
in Diocletian's reorganization of the empire she became
an independent province (*Provincia Tripolitana*), or that
the *dux* and *præses* to whom her military and civil
administration were now respectively entrusted, were
closely subordinated to the highly centralized government of Constantine. The disease of Roman civilization was too deep-seated to be reached by institutional
remedies of that kind. Crushed by taxation on their
own fields, or reduced to serfdom on the ever expanding estates of the large landowners, the peasants had
begun to abandon agriculture on which the material
well-being of the ancient world was based; and all the

spiritual values of classical civilization had been challenged by Christianity which was itself too divided by schism to become—as Constantine tried to make it—a new principle of imperial unity. St. Cyprian, himself an African, draws a sombre picture of the times. « The world itself » he says « now bears witness to its approaching end by the evidence of its failing powers. There is not so much rain in winter for fertilizing the seeds, nor in summer is there so much warmth for ripening them. The springtime is no longer so mild, nor the autumn so rich in fruit. Less marble is quarried from the exhausted mountains, and the dwindling supplies of gold and silver show that the mines are worked out... The peasant is failing and disappearing from the fields, the sailor at sea, the soldier in the camp, uprightness in the forum, justice in the court, concord in friendships, skill in the arts, discipline in morals ».

In the misery of the declining empire Tripolitania had her full share. As early as the end of the third century a Sirtic tribe called the Hilaguas rose in revolt; and it is symptomatic of the general loss of control that the Roman expedition sent to quell the rising failed in its purpose and did not repeat the attempt. But worse was to come. In A.D. 363 the Austurians—a more formidable enemy whose origin is unknown, but who seem to have migrated into Tripolitania from the south —fell on Leptis, plundering and devastating the countryside, burning the farms and killing or taking prisoner their inhabitants. Leptis itself was saved for the moment by its recently rebuilt walls and the Austurians withdrew with their booty. But the terrified citizens fearing their return appealed for aid to Count Romanus, the commander-in-chief of the African garrison. Romanus, in whom the apathy and cynical indifference of the later empire were personified, probably never had any intention of acting in earnest; but he came to Leptis where he demanded as the condition of his help a great quantity of provisions and 4,800 camels which the city was quite unable to provide. The disillusioned citizens next turned to Rome itself. An embassy, on which Oea and Sabratha were represented, was sent to put Tripolitania's case before the emperor, Valentinian I; but Romanus' influence extended to the imperial court and the embassy's representations fell on stony ground. Meanwhile in A.D. 365 the Austurians came again, widening the sphere of their devastation to Oea and Sabratha, of which the latter at all events · was partly destroyed. In desperation the Tripolitanians despatched a second embassy to Valentinian who was finally prevailed upon to send a special legate, Palladius to report on the state of the country. But even Palladius' visit did the Tripolitanians more harm than good. While he was still on his way a third and still more terrible incursion ravaged the unhappy country, and when he came he soon succumbed to the wiles of Count Romanus who bought or extorted from him a report which laid all the blame for the disasters on the victims themselves. If the Austurians now ceased from their invasions it was not for fear of Roman arms. It was because there was little left to rob.

While the barbarians were hammering on Tripolitania from without, the country was being torn within by the religious dissensions which followed the official recognition of Christianity in the Edict of Milan (A.D. 313). Christianity had reached North Africa at an early date and made rapid and remarkable progress there, particularly at Carthage. In Tripolitania a bishop of Leptis is recorded by the end of the second century, and bishops of Leptis, Oea and Sabratha are mentioned in a list drawn up for the council of Carthage in A.D. 256. But the unity which had been the church's strength in the days of its outlawry and persecution, was dissolved by its triumph; and latent differences became open schisms. In Africa the church was sharply divided on the question of the readmission to the Christian community of those who had lapsed during the persecutions and handed over sacred books to the imperial authorities to be burned. The catholic and Roman party held that such persons should be reinstated if repentant: a view uncompromisingly rejected by the schismatic party of the Donatists (so called from one of their leaders, Donatus). But spiritual issues were soon overshadowed by political ones. So long as Christianity had been persecuted by the Roman government, it had rallied to itself anti-Roman discontents of every kind. But now orthodox catholic Christianity had gone far towards identifying itself with the State and oppression; or so it seemed to the ruined and depressed classes of North Africa and to the ever restive natives of the interior. In Donatism they found what they had formerly found in the undivided church—the expression of their non-conformity. They transformed it into a militant political opposition; at times they perverted it into mere banditry at the expense of peaceful citizens, as in the case of the Donatist sect known as the Circumcelliones who ranged over North Africa plundering and pillaging at will and punctuating their acts of violence with cries of « glory be to God ». Donatism found fertile ground in war-torn Tripolitania and of the Tripolitanian bishops attending the council of Carthage in A.D. 411 (at which the heresy was formally condemned) those of Leptis and Oea were both Donatist while only Sabratha sent a Catholic.

The Donatists, who had supported the unsuccessful but bloody Mauretanian revolts of Firmus and Gildo towards the end of the fourth century, found a more powerful ally to help them at the beginning of the fifth. In A.D. 429 King Genseric of the Vandals (a Nordic people who had migrated from Germany to Spain) was invited to cross into Africa by the Roman governor, Count Boniface, who wanted Vandal help against the Empress Placidia. Genseric came—he had been waiting for an opportunity to set foot in Africa—and soon established excellent relations with the Donatists who greeted the Arian Vandals as natural allies in the struggle against Rome and Catholicism. But when a year later the quarrel between Boniface and Placidia came to an end and Boniface tried to rid himself of Genseric and his hordes, the King of the Vandals was in no mood to go; efforts to throw him out by force failed; and finally it was Boniface himself who was compelled to flee the country. With his flight the rule of Rome in Africa came to an end.

xi. THE VANDALS AND BYZANTINES.

Tripolitania, however, was not claimed as part of the Vandal kingdom for another twenty-five years (A.D. 455), when the Vandals seem to have occupied it more by accident than by design. Certainly the country can have had little economic attraction for them. Its agriculture which depended so closely on specialized and scientific methods of cultivation, had been destroyed by the wars and social upheavals of the fourth century. Its commerce had been ruined by the interruption of trade routes and the disappearance of the markets it supplied. Its cities were half deserted and Leptis had already begun to be invaded by sand. But it is curious that the Vandals should have had so little conception of the country's strategic significance as to leave it virtually unguarded. Small garrisons may have been stationed at a few points along the coast; and some importance seems to have been attached to the harbour of Oea since that city was apparently allowed to keep its walls when Leptis and Sabratha lost theirs. But no attempt was made to reorganize the country's frontiers or to defend it with adequate forces; and when the Vandals' hold on it was challenged, they could offer no serious resistance.

The first challenge came from the Byzantine heirs of the eastern Roman empire who formed the ambitious project of recovering for Byzantium all the vast territories lost by Rome in the west. In A.D. 468, under the emperor Leo I, an expedition led by Heraclius had little difficulty in driving the Vandals out of Tripolitania; but it was an ephemeral conquest, for the defeat of a naval expedition sent simultaneously to Tunisia obliged Heraclius to withdraw three years later; and the Byzantines did not repeat their attempt for another sixty years. The Vandals, however, refused to profit by experience and continued to neglect Tripolitania as before. Its defencelessness was a constant invitation to the barbarians of the interior whose invasions grew more dangerous and more disastrous as their conviction of the Vandals' incompetence increased; and when during the reign of the Vandal king Trasamund (A.D. 496-522) the revolt of a number of Tripolitanian tribes under Cabaon, a native chieftain, reached such proportions that not even the Vandals could afford to ignore it, the expedition they sent against the rebels was soundly defeated. A few years later the Leuatha (probably the same people as the Hilaguas) were able to sack Leptis undisturbed and the city was left almost deserted.

The Vandal empire was thus already fast crumbling when in A.D. 533 the Byzantine emperor Justinian revived the project of Leo I and launched an expedition to reconquer North Africa for Eastern Rome and Catholicism. On the eve of the expedition, of which news had probably gone before, a great part of Tripolitania under the leadership of an energetic Tripolitanian, Pudentius, rose against the Vandals and declared its loyalty to the Byzantine emperor who was asked for immediate aid. A force was despatched with the Byzantine general Tattimuth in command and had no difficulty in holding off Vandal attempts at reoccupation until the main expedition reached Tunisia. There in two battles (September and December 533) Belisarius decisively defeated the Vandals and the surrender of King Gelimer marked the end of their remarkable kingdom in North Africa.

The defeat of the Vandals, however, did not bring peace to the Byzantines. The native tribes, which had been passive spectators of the struggle between the old and the new intruders, now rose against the victors. Tattimuth and Pudentius were beseiged by the Leuatha in Leptis and Belisarius was obliged to send them help; but more serious revolts broke out in Numidia and Tunisia which were only with difficulty subdued by Belisarius' successor, Salomon. The uneasy peace which followed was broken in 544 by an episode which took place in Leptis itself. At Leptis there had assembled eighty-one chieftains of the Tripolitanian tribes to do homage to Sergius, a nephew of Salomon who had been appointed military governor of Tripolitania and had already caused considerable discontent by his maladministration. The chieftains were invited by Sergius to attend a banquet within the city; during which, by accident or design, an incident occurred and the Byzantine guards fell on the guests leaving only one to escape alive. The massacre was the signal for a general revolt of the Tripolitanian tribes who, led by the Leuatha, laid siege to Leptis. Driven off at first, the attackers returned in larger numbers and it was not until he had received reinforcements from Carthage that Sergius was able to raise the seige. In the battle Pudentius lost his life.

Meanwhile the revolt had spread to Numidia and Tunisia. Helped by the incompetence of Byzantine anarchy reigning in the Byzantine army and even by the short-lived treason of the *dux* of Numidia himself, the rebels went from strength to strength; and they had only lack of unity to blame for their failure to seize the whole of North Africa before the providential discovery of a capable general saved the situation for the Byzantines.

John Troglita had already served as *dux* of Tripolitania when he was appointed commander-in-chief of all the Byzantine forces in North Africa at the end of 546. His first move was to march against the Tripolitanian tribes, particularly the Leuatha and Austurians, whom he rightly judged to be prime movers in the rebellion. In the ensuing battle the natives were routed and their leader, the Leuathan Jerna, fell on the field. But remnants of the shattered army managed to escape to the south where they reorganized and gained the support of the Nasamones and Garamantes before marching once more against the coast. Although it was the height of summer John immediately set out to meet the rebels, but as he approached they retired and his troops, refusing to follow an elusive enemy through the heat of the desert, turned back towards Tunisia. The enemy, however, followed closely in their footsteps and choosing their moment fell upon them unexpectedly and inflicted a severe defeat. John was obliged to abandon Tripolitania to the rebels' mercy while he himself withdrew to Tunisia to reconstitute his army. It was not long, however, before he was again prepared for battle and this time the result was final. Besieged in an entrenched position they had taken up in southern Tunisia, the enemy tried to break out and were completely routed after a short engagement. It was the last rebellion in Byzantine Tripolitania which now enjoyed a century of peace until the Arab invasion of A.D. 643.

During their wars with the natives the Byzantines had done something to reorganize the administration and defence of Africa. In their treatment of Tripolitania they did not repeat the Vandals' mistake of neglect. It became one of the seven provinces into which Africa was divided, and was placed under the governorship of a *rector consularis* assisted by a committee of fifty members. Leptis (which was chosen as the seat of the government) and Sabratha were refortified, though their new walls enclosed only a small part of the Roman cities, so greatly had their populations dwindled by now. The *Limes Tripolitanus* was rebuilt in part and Belisarius himself, before leaving Africa, revived the Severan plan of stationing soldier-farmers to guard strategic points.

It was the avowed intention of Justinian to restore Catholicism in North Africa after its long subordination to the Arian Vandals and their Donatist allies. When the pacification of the native tribes had been completed, an ambitious programme of evangelization was undertaken in the interior of the country. Procopius, a contemporary historian, informs us that the Gadabitani (an otherwise unknown tribe probably inhabiting the Jebel), the people of Cydamus and even the Garamantes of the Fezzan were converted to Catholicism by the Byzantines; and ruins of Christian churches, which appear to be connected with this period, have been found as far south as the Wadi Soffegin. In the coastal cities, also, new churches were built and Procopius mentions in particular a stately church dedicated to the Mother of God at Leptis and another notable church at Sabratha.

But neither the Byzantine administrative reforms nor the restoration of Catholicism could suffice to bring back more than a shadow of life to the spent province. Taxed no less heavily than under the later Roman empire, the human and natural resources of the country were less than ever able to bear the burden. Soil erosion and a diminution of the rainfall (small perhaps, but critical) were probably already fast completing the work of desolation which the barbarian invasions had begun. The greater part of the population, the native and Donatist element, seems to have maintained an attitude of sullen apathy towards their new rulers, while the Byzantines themselves had no constructive policy to offer with which to enlist their support. It is almost as if they realized from the beginning the impermanence and artificiality of their dominion and had neither the confidence nor the energy to consolidate it. When the Arabs came they found little organized resistance. Only the stubborn tribesmen, withdrawing to their hills, remained to dispute for a long time yet the possession of their native land.

PART II

GUIDE TO THE
PRINCIPAL MONUMENTS

i. LEPTIS MAGNA.

(Numbers in brackets refer to plan opposite)

General Remarks.

Although no traces of Phœnician Leptis have so far been discovered, it was certainly situated on the left bank of the mouth of the Wadi Lebda in the unexcavated area to the northeast of the Old Forum (15). Its cemetery, which was probably well outside the town, lay where the Roman theatre (25) now stands. Under the Romans Leptis begins to develop on the rectangular layout characteristic of Roman town planning. The Augustan city seems to have enclosed the area southwest of the Old Forum perhaps as far as the Market (21), but the Theatre, although of Augustan date, is thought to have been built outside the city limits. By the middle of the first century, however, it had been included by a rapid expansion of the city which now reached as far as the point where the Arch of Septimius Severus (2) was later built. In the first half of the second century the Great Baths (5) were built in the area between the southern extremity of the city and the Wadi Lebda, which must already have been dammed to prevent flooding of the site. At the end of this century the great Severan building programme filled the remaining vacant space between the wadi and the city with the architectural complex of the new Forum and Basilica (8 and 9) and the Colonnaded Street (7) leading from the Great Baths to the Harbour (10), which is also probably a Severan creation in its present form. By this time the Circus and Amphitheatre had already been built on the other side of the wadi and a continuous line of buildings connected them with the harbour along the seashore. Further inland on this side the topography is uncertain owing to lack of excavation, but there is a cemetery area near the main Zliten road. It is estimated that at the height of its development, which it reached under the Severan emperors, Leptis had a population of about eighty thousand. This vast expansion was probably too great for the real needs and capabilities of the city and a rapid decay set in during the second half of the third century which was accelerated in the fourth century when a large area of the city was abandoned to the encroaching sands and only a few approach roads were kept clear by blocking the street doors of uninhabited houses. The contraction continued during the fifth century and when the Byzantines rebuilt the city walls in the first half of the sixth, their perimeter contained little more than the harbour and the two forum areas.

Two main kinds of stone are used for construction. The first is a hard grey limestone from the Ras-el-Hammam quarries which was employed for carved architectural decoration, for surfaces where a good finish was required, and for places where stress or wear would be considerable, as, for example, under columns and for road-paving. The other is a softer sandstone from Ras-el-Mergheb normally used in less conspicuous and less exacting positions. From the second century onwards the use of coloured marbles, imported from all parts of the empire, becomes fashionable for columns, mouldings, veneers for walls and floors and other decorative purposes. Brickwork, in which the curving surfaces of apses and niches were more easily carried out, is characteristic of the Severan age, but it was never left uncovered.

Itinerary.

(The following itinerary for a visit to the excavations of Leptis which includes most of the more important monuments, requires at least four hours to complete satisfactorily; but for the convenience of more hurried visitors certain monuments are marked with an asterisk, from which a shorter itinerary may be compiled).

From the ENTRANCE (1) a path leads down a flight of steps to the level of the ancient southbound road across which at the first intersection stands the *ARCH OF SEPTIMIUS SEVERUS (2) *(Plate 1)*. Erected probably in A.D. 203 or 204 in honour of the emperor, it is a foursided arch of Janus type and was originally covered with eleborate marble decorative and relief sculpture. The four arches were flanked by pairs of Corinthian columns of cipollino marble, each column carrying a small raking half pediment, a device which must have given the monument a decidedly baroque appearance. Most of the relief sculpture has now been collected on the high ground immediately to the southeast of the arch (3). In comparison with the work of earlier periods it shows considerable stylistic innovation in which later developments of Byzantine art are fore-shadowed. Particularly noteworthy in this connection is the black-and-white effect of the deep undercutting on some of the pilasters showing birds and figures entwined in vinescrolls. Other reliefs present historical scenes (triumph of Septimius Severus; Septimius shaking his son, Caracalla, by the hand in the presence of Geta and the tutelary deities of Leptis; siege of a city, etc.) in which the tendency to frontality, the turning of the eyes towards the spectator and the linear grouping of the figures betray a conscious reaction from classical realism (e.g. the triumphal scene illustrated in *Plate 2*). Notice also the strongly stylized winged victories from the spandrels.

Turning right at the arch and taking the first (and only excavated) turning to the left the visitor reaches the PALÆSTRA or sports ground (4), a large straight-sided open space with semicircular ends and surrounded by a portico of Corinthian columns of cipollino marble. Abutting on its southern side, though on a slightly more westerly axis, are the *GREAT BATHS (5) erected in A.D. 123-127 under the emperor Hadrian and restored and redecorated under Commodus (A.D. 180-192). Their plan (which may be seen on the wall beyond the swimming pool) is symmetrical along the north-south axis. At the northeast and northwest corners are changing-rooms (*apodyteria*) and lavatories; in the centre of the north side lies the *natatio*, or open swimming bath, surrounded on three sides by columns of pink breccia marble. From the *natatio* a doorway leads across a corridor into the central hall (*cella media*), a large room originally covered by three cross-vaults carried on eight Corinthian columns of cipollino. Two small cold baths (*frigidaria*) with marble decoration and black granite columns lie symmetrically to either side *(Plate 3)*. South of the central hall comes the *Tepidarium* or warm room with a bath to either side and one (colonnaded) in the centre; and finally the *Calidarium* or hot room with hot baths round the sides. Two doors to either side of the north wall of the *Calidarium* lead into the *Laconia* or sweat baths where the raised flooring and hollow bricks for the circulation of heat are clearly visible. Round the outside of the *Calidarium* were arranged the heating furnaces, though their disposition is not entirely plain. Apart from architectural decoration the baths were ornamented with many statues, Roman copies of Greek originals, some of which may be seen in the museum.

The east end of the Palæstra gives on to a circular open space on the opposite side of which may be seen the GREAT NYMPHÆUM (6), a large and elaborate decorative fountain built in the Severan period. It consisted of a semicircular apse formed in a massive rectangular core of brickwork and conglomerate (half of which has fallen) and decorated with marble veneer and two (possibly originally three) superimposed rows of columns, an architectural scheme recalling the treatment of the back wall of theatre stages (see the theatres of Leptis and Sabratha). The screen ornamented with carved heads which stands in front of the Nymphæum, is a later addition.

To the northeast of the Nymphæum and approached through arched entrances extends the magnificent Severan *COLONNADED STREET (7) flanked on either side throughout its length by covered porticos of cipollino columns carrying a continuous arcading. Note the unusual capitals of so-called Pergamene style, many of which may be seen lying on the ground.

Following this street the visitor passes on the left a series of small compartments, probably shops, lining the south wall of the *FORUM NOVUM SEVERIANUM or new Severan forum (8), which is entered by a large door in the centre of this side. The forum and associated basilica are the principal monuments of the Severan age in Leptis and in the grandeur of their conception and the interest of their workmanship they are unsurpassed by any other constructions of their kind in the Roman world with the exception of Rome itself. The forum, which has an area of some 10,000 square metres, was surrounded by a single-storied portico of cipollino columns carrying a continuous arcading with carved Medusa and Nereid heads between the arches. The capitals have the same form as those of the Colonnaded Street. On the arcading lay a richly carved frieze of foliage scroll in black-and-white technique (it is now laid out along the south side of the forum) and a terrace roof connected the entablature to the wall behind the portico. All the internal walls were covered with marble panelling. At the west end of the forum rises the *podium* or base of a large temple which is believed by some to have been dedicated to Septimius Severus. A broad flight of steps, interrupted in the centre by an entrance to the crypt, led up to the three-sided portico of red granite columns by which the *cella* (the main chamber of the temple) was surrounded. Some of the columns in front rested on pedestals carved with scenes depicting battles of the giants. At the opposite end of the forum *(Plate 4)* a line of irregularly-shaped rooms serves to mask a difference in the orientation of the forum and basilica, arising from the exigencies of the earlier street plan on the northern side. An apse-like exhedra in the centre of these rooms, and the most northerly room itself, give access to the *BASILICA SEVE-RIANA (9) by which the earlier basilica or law-court in the Old Forum was replaced under Septimius Severus, the building being finished in A.D. 216 under his successor, Caracalla. The basilica *(Plate 5)* is divided into nave and aisles by two rows of Corinthian columns of red Egyptian granite, on which stood a second row of columns supporting a wooden roof. Galleries running along the sides above the aisles were reached by staircases built into the thickness of the walls of the two end apses. The apses, in which the judges sat on a raised floor, were lined with a semicircle of cipollino columns and flanked by a pair of carved pilasters on either side.

Of these pilasters *(Plate 6)* some are carved in foliage spirals among which human and animal figures appear, the forepart of an animal often forming the centre of a rosette. Other pilasters show Bacchic subjects and the Labours of Hercules, the various scenes being linked together by vine scrolls. Stylistically the carving is of great importance for its strong development of the black-and-white tendencies already noticed on other Severan reliefs. In some of the present examples the figures and foliage are almost completely detached from the background and have the appearance of openwork rather than relief sculpture. Their inspiration is certainly eastern (perhaps from Aphrodisias in Asia Minor) and is not generally felt in the west until Byzantine times.

At each side of the two apses are irregularly shaped chambers, by means of which the basilica conforms to the street plan outside. They have been considerably altered from their original state and the northwest chamber, which contains a cruciform font for total immersion, formed the baptistry of the church into which the basilica was transformed in the Byzantine period and which is perhaps to be identified with the church of the Mother of God mentioned by Procopius. Other evidence of this transformation may be seen in the pulpit (formed of a split capital of the Severan arch) and in the screens in front of the south apse (formed of pilasters from the same source) which enclosed the presbytery.

A good general view of the excavations may be had from the top of the staircase built into the north apse; and before leaving the basilica area the visitor is recommended to look at the massive plain wall of the northern exterior of the forum and basilica, and the colonnaded eastern exterior of the basilica, both of which may be reached by a door in the latter.

Continuing along the Colonnaded Street the PORT (10) is reached after passing the remains of a smaller nymphæum on the left. The Port, which in its present form is probably largely a construction of the Severan period, is polygonal in shape and has a total circuit of about three-quarters of a mile (of which only the two seaward extremities have been excavated). The basin itself is almost completely silted up except where it is crossed by the Wadi Lebda. Disregarding the quayside arrangements which are better studied on the eastern side of the harbour, the visitor should proceed at once to the end of the western spit where, partly resting on huge stone blocks by which, it seems, an existing reef was enlarged to receive it, stands the LIGHTHOUSE (11), a rectangular construction of masonry and conglomerate entered by a flight of steps on the landward side. The western and northern sides have fallen into the sea, but enough remains to reconstruct the symmetrical plan of the original building which even in ruin remains one of the most impressive monuments of Leptis.

Returning a short distance from the lighthouse the harbour mouth may be crossed on a sand-bar which now links one side with the other. At the end of the eastern mole *(Plate 7)* stand a watchtower with an internal stone staircase; and an attractive small DORIC TEMPLE (12) with an altar in front of its once colonnaded porch and a continuous pedestal for statuary across its internal back wall. On the seaward side of these two buildings may be seen the remains of the Byzantine wall, in the perimeter of which the harbour was included: it is built almost entirely from reused materials. In this area of the harbour the waterside arrangements are particularly clear. The quays are built in straight runs and stepped back to form two levels, the lower being at the water's edge and probably at its height. In the vertical face of the higher level are set pierced stone mooring blocks and staircase to connect the two levels. Along the top ran a portico behind which lay warehouses, chandlers' stores, etc. The southwest margin of the harbour (which may be approached from here directly, or may be conveniently included in a visit to the Circus—see page 75 below) is differently treated, consisting of a long continuous flight of small steps leading up from the water's edge. That it was not used for shipping is almost certain from the presence on it of a large TEMPLE (13) (perhaps dedicated to Jove Dolichenus, though the evidence is not conclusive). Only the broad front steps and part of the *podium* have been excavated, but the exceptionally large proportions of the building are evident from the size of the mound by which the rest is covered.

Returning across the harbour mouth and along the

western quays the visitor will find a footpath branching off to the right across the area occupied by the pre-Roman city (many unexcavated Roman remains are also visible). and leading to the *CURIA, or meeting chamber of the city magistrates (14). Standing within a colonnaded courtyard entered on the southwest side by a broad flight of steps, the chamber itself is a temple-like structure standing on a *podium* with a porch of cipollino columns in front, to which a second staircase gives access from the courtyard. Inside may be seen remains of the broad, shallow steps on which the magistrates' seats were placed. The building appears to date from the late first or early second century.

Immediately west of the Curia lies the *OLD FORUM (15, *Plate 8*), the centre of the city's religious and administrative life until it was replaced by the Severan forum and probably even then retaining much of its traditional prestige. In its present form it dates substantially from the early imperial period; remains of an Augustan paving may be seen in the northwest corner where some flags still preserve the marks of an inlaid bronze inscription recording the name of Cn. Calpurnius Piso. The rest of the paving, however, was laid down in the reign of Claudius (A.D. 41-54) and is commemorated in the four inscriptions in front of the main temple (19). A semicircular seat surmounted by statues was set up in the forum in honour of Septimius Severus; and the Byzantines built a baptistery in the middle.

Around the forum stood the most important public buildings of the city. On the southeast side lay the OLD BASILICA, or law-court (16), a long rectangular hall divided longitudinally by two rows of columns into a nave and two aisles, and entered by two doors in the short northeast end; across the southwest end were situated five adjoining rooms of which the central one, larger than the others, presumably contained the judges' dais. The original construction, which is earlier than the Claudian forum, underwent considerable alteration at a later date, possibly in the fourth century, when the earlier columns were replaced by smaller columns of black granite.

The southern end of the southwest side of the forum is occupied by a little temple dedicated to Cybele, the Great Mother, which stood in a colonnaded courtyard behind a portico. Next to it, on the same side, and separated from it by a street lies the *CHRISTIAN BASILICA (17) on the site of an earlier building, remains of which are incorporated in its structure. For the rest of the basilica materials from other earlier buildings (including much Trajanic architectural ornament) were used. It is of rectangular form with a semicircular apse (contained within straight external walls) at the northeast end, and nave and aisles are separated by two rows of paired granite columns. A porch or *narthex*, overlying an earlier street, occupied the full width of the southwest end; and the area near the more northerly of the two doors flanking the apse was used as a Christian burial ground. One of the funeral inscriptions records an unhappy father's loss of three sons in three days, probably as the result of an epidemic.

A three-sided marble-paved portico lies at the west angle of the forum between the Christian Basilica and the large *TEMPLE OF LIBER PATER (18) of which the front steps and a large part of the *podium* survive. The complicated system of interconnecting crypts which surround the solid centre of the *podium* is clearly visible. On top of the solid part was built the rectangular *cella* or temple-chamber, the surrounding colonnade of fluted white marble columns with Corinthian capitals being carried on the crypt walls. A fragment of the inlaid marble floor of the *cella* is preserved in position. The temple is probably early imperial in origin, though the marble decoration is a later addition. It is difficult to believe that the poor quality sandstone of which even the external walls of the *podium* are constructed, was left uncovered in places where it would have been visible, but there are no traces of stucco or marble veneering. The dedication to Liber Pater or Bacchus, one of the patron deities of Leptis with whom a Phœnician god was identified, is probable but not proven.

Next to this temple, and subsequently joined to it by a platform carried on arches over the intervening road, stands the chief temple of the forum which is believed to have been the *TEMPLE OF ROME AND AUGUSTUS* (19). Behind the Byzantine wall, by which the rear of the building has been intersected, may be seen the two limestone half-columns with Ionic capitals which stood at the return ends of the colonnade surrounding the sides and front of the *cella*. The half-columns appear to have been joined together across the back of the temple by a plain wall. Of the rest of the temple only the crypts survive, the long lateral ones being originally lighted by windows which were later partly masked by the arches of the platform already mentioned. An inscription in Phœnician on the lintel of the *cella* door (now lying on the ground in front of the temple) gives the date of dedication as between A.D. 14 and 19. At a later period the *podium* was extended forwards by the addition of a platform for public orators, to which access is given by two lateral staircases. That this was done under Claudius is almost certainly proved by the inscriptions of Claudian date set up in front of the platform (one survives *in situ* and though it has lost its bronze letters their imprints are clearly legible).

From the ruins of these two temples comes the impressive series of portrait sculptures of the Julio-Claudian emperors and their families, some of which may be seen in the museum.

North of the Temple of Rome and Augustus, and possibly connected to it by another platform, lies a smaller temple of unknown dedication in which were found several inscriptions in honour of Septimius Severus and his family; but its elevation and architectural decoration are still very doubtful. A portico with a large unexcavated building behind occupied the northeast side of the forum.

Leaving the forum by the street between the Christian Basilica and the Temple of Cybele the visitor comes to the BYZANTINE GATE (20) which formed the only known entrance in Justinian's walls. It is constructed of re-used materials from earlier buildings including many fragments of inscriptions. From the gate the street continues with a slight change of axis between rectangular blocks of unexcavated buildings, probably mainly first century shops and private houses, until the *MARKET (21) is reached on the right-hand side. This is a large rectangular enclosure with a colonnade of Corinthian columns of black granite running round all four sides. In the centre stood two circular kiosks surrounded by octagonal porticos, on the entablature of which rested a wooden roof. The northern one, which has been recently restored and makes an attractive small building, was constructed of limestone. Between the columns of its portico (which show an interesting solution of the angle problem) may be seen some of the counters on which meat, fish, vegetables and cereals were sold, as well as measures. Of the other kiosk, which was in marble, little more than the foundation remains. Between the two a small four-sided arch decorated with ships in relief (probably third century) records the gift to Leptis of four live elephants by one, Porphyrius, a dealer in livestock for the amphitheatre. The market is probably Augustan in origin, as is suggested by a dedicatory inscription in Phœnician dated 8 B.C., but much of the building, including the portico and marble kiosk must be later restoration or addition.

Returning to the street the visitor comes at once upon the small undecorated single ARCH OF TIBERIUS (2) dedicated during the proconsulship of C. Rubellius Blandus and under the supervision of his legate M. Etrilius Lupercus. The inscription commemorates the paving of the streets of Leptis from « the income deriving from the lands restored to the citizens of Leptis »; and since it dates from A.D. 35-36, it seems likely that the lands referred to are those rescued by Roman troops from the Garamantes during the revolt of Tacfarinas (A.D. 16-24). A similar arch with the same inscription stood across a street just north of the theatre and it is probable that the streets which were now paved, lay to the south of a line joining the two arches, in a part of the town only systematically developed after the Augustan period.

A little further along the same street, at an intersection, stands the four-sided ARCH OF TRAJAN (23) dedicated in A.D. 110 during the proconsulship of Q. Pomponius Rufus, though its construction seems to have been decreed or begun by the proconsul C. Cornelius Rarus Sextius. Rufus' legate, L. Asinius

Rufus was responsible for the building. Unlike the Tiberian arches this Trajanic examples has a decorative as well as a commemorative function; its limestone ornament (including fluted Corinthian columns: two on each external face and one in each internal angle) shows an admirable sobriety and precision of carving.

Immediately next to Trajan's Arch, on the right-hand side of the street, stands a building which, from a thrice repeated inscription (now laid out along the top of the porch steps) appears to be a CHALCIDICUM (24). The meaning of this word is, however, doubtful. At times it appears to be used of a room, usually irregular in plan, by which one part of a building is adapted to another on a different axis (cf. the various compartments of the Severan Forum). But it is also possible that it designates a market for textiles and similar goods. However that may be, the general form of the present building is clear in spite of considerable later additions and alterations. It consisted of a portico of cipollino columns running along the top of a broad flight of steps (at either end of which cisterns were added in a late period). Behind the portico and in the centre of a row of shops lay a small temple or shrine (in which the base for a cult-statue may still be seen); while behind these again a large rectangular open space surrounded by porticos perhaps formed part of the same complex. Some of the columns of the southwest side of this enclosure may be seen built into the wall of a large late water-tank which has also engulfed a second row of larger columns, apparently part of the same portico. According to the inscription already mentioned the Chalcidicum dates from A.D. 11-12 and was built at the expense of Iddibal Caphada Aemilius, a Phœnician citizen. But the front colonnade in its present form appears to be later than this date, while the central shrine is perhaps earlier than the main structure.

The street flanking the southwest side of the Chalcidicum leads to the THEATRE (25) which was built and dedicated ˌin A.D. 1-2 by another Phœnician citizen, Annobal Rufus, who commemorates his not unselfconscious munificence (« embellisher of his country » he calls himself) in three inscriptions each in Latin and Phœnician. Subsequent enlargements and decorative additions were made in the course of the next two centuries. The lowest rows of the *cavea* or auditorium *(Plate 9)* are largely cut in the virgin rock, an artificial mound of earth and stone supports the middle rows, and the highest rest on massive piers of stone and concrete. Round the top of the *cavea*, behind the highest row of seats, ran a semicircular colonnade interrupted in the centre by a temple dedicated to Ceres-Tyche, a combination of the divinities of vegetation and good fortune). The massive outside wall of the auditorium is undecorated save for a simple moulding and plain pilasters and is broken only by the arched entrances of five radial passages leading to the middle rows of seats. The highest rows were reached from the inside by staircases leading up between the seats themselves; but two further entrance passages led down between the auditorium and the stage to the lowest seats where the most distinguished spectators sat. The front of the stage was decorated with niches containing statues of divinities, while at its back rose the ornamental wall *(scaenae frons)* which provided the unchanging backcloth of Roman drama. It was recessed to form three semicircular exhedræ, each containing an entrance, and was decorated in the second half of the second century with statues and three superimposed rows of coloured marble columns. Behind the stage and certainly connected with the theatre lies an irregularly quadrilateral enclosure surrounded by a portico with marble panelled walls and containing, among other monuments, a small temple dedicated to the *Dei Augusti* (the deified emperors) and a statue base with an inscription in honour of the actor M. Septimius Aurelius Agrippa, « the best turn of his day ».

Other Monuments at Leptis.

For those who still have time to spare, Leptis possesses other monuments and a museum, all well worth visiting. The most important of the monuments not included in the itinerary given above are the Circus and adjacent unexcavated Amphitheatre, the fourth century Wall and Gate and a small bathing establishment by the sea to the west of the excavated area. The CIRCUS (not on the plan) lies along the shore about half a mile east of the Wadi Lebda and may be reached by a road leaving the main road just east of the wadi bridge. Measuring 450 by 100 metres it is one of the largest circuses known, though only a small part of the northeast end has been uncovered. Here the seats may be seen and one of the semicircular turning points. The *spina* or dividing line down the middle of the course was formed by five long basins of water instead of the more normal wall.

The FOURTH CENTURY WALLS AND GATE (26) and the small bathing establishment may conveniently be visited together. The gate incorporates in its structure a marble decorated triumphal arch, probably of the early second century, of which the general design is plainly visible. On either side of it the fourth century builders added semi-circular flanking towers constructed, as is the rest of the wall, from re-used materials. The SMALL BATHS (27), of which the key should be obtained at the museum, are remarkable for the preservation of their vaulted and domed roofs (prototypes of Berber architecture) and for the succession of period which can be traced in their painted and mosaic decoration. In the first covered room (*frigidarium*) there is a notable painting of scenes from the amphitheatre, and remains of mosaics may be seen in the half-domes of the basins in the end-walls. The plunge bath, on to which the northern wall of this room opens, is not part of the original plan and its left side incorporates half of an earlier barrel-vaulted room, the other half of which may be seen outside. Beyond the *frigidarium* are two octagonal domed chambers, one giving access to a private bathing suite, the other probably the *tepidarium* or warm bath and leading into the two *calidaria* or hot baths.

The MUSEUM (28) contains sculpture and mosaics found in the excavations, some of which have already been mentioned. Many of the statues are lifeless copies of Greek originals possessing only a remote academic interest; but a powerful head of an old woman (known to the Italians as the « mother-in-law of Leptis »), an overlifesize figure of a young magistrate *(Plate 10)* and a headless and limbless female torso are all works with original qualities of their own. Notice also a competent if cold little head of the Emperor Hadrian and a strange mosaic from the so-called Villa of the Nile showing the toilet of the winged horse Pegasus. Other objects of interest are a stone elephant (a reflection probably of the city's export of these beasts for the amphitheatre), three torsos of warriors usually held to be Phœnician carvings, and an inscription found in the baths attached to the Severan fort of Bu Ngem (see below p. 105). The inscription was erected by a centurion, Q. AVIDIVS QVINTIANVS, whose name is given acrostically by the first letter of each line of the poem he wrote to record the fact that the swimming bath was his gift to the camp. It runs in rough translation:

I've pondered long how best commemorate—
Acting for every soldier in this camp—
Our common prayer and hope of safe return
To see our old folk and our sons to be.
While looking for a worthy god, at last
I found a goddess fit in name and nature
To be enshrined here in continual prayers.
HEALTH, then, 's the name I've done my best
                               [to make
Holy while her cult lasts; to all I've given
Health's genuine waters, so that when the heat
Beats on these endless dunes, they may relax
And find relief in swimming from the sun's
And fitful ghibli's scorching. So if you
Feel really grateful for my work when your
Spirit revives within the seething breast,
Then don't neglect to sound the honest praise
Of him who wished you fit for your own good
But shout it out—and so please Health as well. (

WATER SUPPLY.

Some of the most interesting Roman remains of
Leptis are those connected with the city's water supply.
To provide water for a city with a population of sixty
to eighty thousand and a passion for baths and fountains
was no mean feat in a country as poor in natural water
resources as Tripolitania; and although the system by
which it was achieved is still far from being fully
understood, its ambitious scale is well illustrated by the
remains of the aqueduct which brought water to the city
from the Wadi Caam twelve miles away, and by the two
large reservoirs in the Wadi Lebda south of the city.
The aqueduct is most easily seen by walking two hundred yards down the left bank of the Wadi Caam from
the main Homs-Zliten road. It consists of a large
cement-lined conduit (sunk in the ground for most of

(1)   Quæsii multum quot memoriæ tradere
      Agens præ cunctos in hac castra milites
      Votum communem proque reditu exercitus
      Inter priores et futuros reddere
      Dum quæro mecum digna divom nomina
      Inveni tandem nomen et numen deæ
      Votis perennem quem dicare in hoc loco
      Salutis igitur quamdiu cultores sient
      Qua potui sanxi nomen et cunctis dedi
      Veras salutis lymphas tantis ignibus
      In istis semper harenacis collibus
      Nutantis austri solis flammas fervidas
      Tranquille ut nando delenirent corpora
      Ita tu qui sentis magnam facti gratiam
      Aestuantis animæ fucilari spiritum
      Noli pigere laudem voce reddere
      Veram qui voluit esse te sanum tibi
      Set protestare ve salutis gratia.

its length and perhaps working on the siphon principle) with hollow square pillars built on top of it at frequent intervals, apparently to give access for cleaning purposes or inspection. Originally it spanned the wadi and the continuation of it can be seen on the right bank where it enters a massive containing wall running parallel to the course of the stream. Remains of other barrages may be seen further down the wadi and it appears likely that the whole river basin in this area was dammed and built up to form a reservoir. It is still fed by a perennial stream which issues from the side of an apparently artificially excavated pool close to, but not easily seen from, the main road. Whether, as would seem logical, the water so collected was fed into the aqueduct, and if so, how, it is impossible to say.

The aqueduct is believed to have supplied the northernmost of two reservoirs in the Wadi Lebda a little way south of the main road. The northern one consists of five parallel vaulted cisterns which discharged into a water-channel leading towards the city. The other reservoir, though smaller, is distinguished by the architectural treatment of its stone façade which is decorated with niches and doorways. The general appearance suggests a Severan date. At the back of the building iron steps give access to the roof from which a good view of the three internal cisterns may be obtained through holes in the vaulting. Notice also the care with which rain falling on the roof was collected, an indication of the anxious conservation of every drop of available water. The source of supply for this reservoir is still undetected, but its outlet seems to have fed the northern reservoir.

About a quarter of a mile further up the wadi are the remains of the great concrete barrage built to divert the stream from its original course through Leptis and so prevent the periodic flooding of the area of the Great Baths and Severan Forum and also the silting up of the harbour. A new bed was dug for the stream carrying it round the western outskirts of the city to the sea. In the course of time the wadi has found its way past the eastern end of the barrage and back into its old bed. A recent flood (October, 1945) provided an excellent illustration of what the Romans had contrived to prevent happening. The barrage is presumably, earlier than the Great Baths (A.D. 127), but has probably had later reinforcements.

ii. OEA (TRIPOLI).

Unlike Leptis and Sabratha, which were abandoned at the end of antiquity and thereafter remained undisturbed until excavated in modern times, the site of Oea has been continuously inhabited from the Phœnician period until the present day, and its ancient buildings have long since been razed to make room for the buildings of later generations. Nevertheless traces of them have been met at various points during demolitions in the area of the Old City. Mosaics and foundations have been found between Bab-el-Gedid and the sea and also in the neighbourhood of the former Spanish Fort which stood on the harbour mole; a Phœnician cemetery of the Roman period has been excavated at the Forte della Vite; and there are remains of what may have been a private house under the new Cassa di Risparmio on the water-front north of the Castello. Under the Castle itself the construction of the docks

tunnel brought to light a network of heavy concrete foundations, some platforms of sandstone blocks, remains of mosaic pavements and a few large cipollino marble columns; all of which suggest that a large public building stood on this spot. One would like to connect it with the basilica capable of holding « an enormous gathering » in which, so Apuleius tells us in his Apology, he delivered his lectures to the Oeans. But the plan, so far as it can be reconstructed at all, shows nothing of the normal basilical layout.

The only Roman building still standing in Tripoli is the ARCH OF MARCUS AURELIUS *(Plate 11)* which lies in an open square facing the harbour towards the north end of the Old City. To what it owes its unique fortune it is difficult to say, but when the Italians occupied Tripoli in 1911 it was undergoing the last and least dignified of a long series of transformations— into a cinema. Except for its sandstone foundations and a cement filling round the outside of the dome, it is built throughout of white Greek marble, an extravagance which distinguishes it at once as a monument of more than ordinary pretentions. In form it is a Janus or four-sided arch of rectangular plan and stood over a cross-roads, part of the original paving of which has survived. A niche for statuary and a free-standing column stood to each side of the arches on the two longer elevations (east and west) which presumably faced on to the more important street. The sculptural decoration is best preserved on the north side, on which, between the angle pilasters of the piers, are represented captive barbarians beneath trophies and in the spandrils of the arches Minerva and Apollo driving chariots drawn by winged griffins. On the east and west sides there were portrait medallions above the niches and winged victories in the spandrils. The octagonal dome is formed of three rings of coffered blocks with a central filling piece, and is adapted to the rectangular plan of the piers by internally projecting courses on the east and west sides. At the same height on the outside of the monument ran a frieze and cornice which on the north face has been carved flat for the greater part of its length to accommodate the dedicatory inscription. Above the cornice there is no structural evidence to show what form the monument took. It is usual for an arch to have a low balustrade in this position and it is on this that the inscription is normally carved. The unusual and make-shift accommodation of the inscription in the present case suggests that the design of the monument was altered after the frieze was in position and that the new design had no balustrade. A seventeenth century painting of Tripoli shows the arch surmounted by a polygonal and domed kiosk with arcaded sides, the substitution of which for the originally intended balustrade would provide a reasonable explanation of the facts. The monument is dated in A.D. 163. It was built in honour of Marcus Aurelius and Lucius Verus (of whom a statue was found in front of one of the niches) at the expense of C. Calpurnius Celsus, a magistrate of the city, and dedicated by the proconsul Sergius Cornelius Scipio Salvidienus Orfitus and his legate Uttedius Marcellus. There can be no question of this being a rededication of an already existing monument, as has been suggested and as might perhaps be inferred from the alteration of the design, for Celsus expressly states in the inscription that he laid the foundations of the arch and built it of solid marble.

During the excavations to lay bare the ancient street level in the same area fragments of the decoration of a temple were discovered which are now to be seen immediately northwest of the Arch. They consist of remains of the entablature and part of a pediment. An inscription on the former gives the date of the temple as A.D. 183-184 and records that it was dedicated by L. Aemilius (?Frontinus) to the Genius of the Colony (Oea). The sculpture of the pediment represents the Genius standing between Minerva and Apollo with one of the twin Dioscuri at the side (his counterpart is missing).

iii. SABRATHA.

General remarks.

Although there is no evidence to indicate the size or limits of the Phœnician city of Sabratha, it may be assumed that it lay close to the sea, probably in the area north of the Forum (5) where the curving and somewhat irregular street plan seems to betray a pre-Roman origin, though the buildings themselves are Roman. The early imperial city was laid out on the general axis given by the Forum (northwest-southeast) with many subordinate variations. How far south it extended cannot be said in the present state of excavation, but the same orientation is still respected by the streets intersecting immediately north of the main entrance (1). In the second half of the second century the theatre (21) was built on a new axis (north-south) and in a hitherto undeveloped area to the east of the earlier city. It formed the nucleus of the more rigidly rectangular layout on which the residential quarter to the north of it was built at much about the same period. Unlike Leptis Sabratha did not produce an emperor (though she produced an emperor's wife: Flavia Domitilla, wife of Vespasian) and was not tempted to outgrow her strength. The little that remains of the fourth century wall (in the area of the Temple of Isis, 19) suggests that on its eastern side at all events the city had not greatly shrunk by that date; and even after the destruction caused by the Austurians (A.D. 365) reconstruction was undertaken on a considerable scale. Sabratha never achieved the splendour of Leptis, but her decline seems to have been more gradual. The fifth century, however, must certainly have seen a rapid decrease in population, for the Byzantine walls enclose a greatly diminished city, from which the whole of the theatre area and a large part of the older city are excluded.

The material mainly used in the construction of Sabratha is an extremely friable sandstone from the quarries immediately southeast of the theatre. To save it from the erosion of salt-laden sea winds it was normally covered by a hard white lime stucco capable of receiving a very smooth finish and well adapted to decorative treatment on mouldings, columns, capitals, etc. The use of marble becomes frequent during the second century, to which date belongs an interesting inscription recording the gift to the city by a rich citizen, Caius Flavius Pudens, of twelve fountains covered with marble panelling (crustœ). But marble is not so lavishly used as at wealthier Leptis and even a certain economy in its employment is suggested by the fact that one of the city's principal buildings (the Antonine Temple, 4) has marble decoration on the front only, the sides and back being rendered in stucco.

The excavations of Sabratha, in contrast to those of Leptis, have disclosed a number of private houses, from which something of the domestic life of the citizens can be learnt. Most of the houses are narrow in plan, suggesting that building space within the city was hard to come by; but they compensate for this to some extent by expanding upwards. Second storeys are common as can be seen from the holes for ceiling beams which occur in many houses, and from the staircases which survive in some. Beneath the ground floor a cistern was often sunk in which rainwater from the roof was collected, the public supply of water probably being on a limited scale. An interesting constructional detail is the prevalence of wooden lintels let into the stonework above doorways, presumably because wood was found to be tougher than the local sandstone. For interior decoration painted stucco was normally used on the walls and mosaics on the floor; many remains of both are to be seen still in their original positions, but the best examples are now in the museum. In the following itinerary one or two houses of special interest are mentioned in passing, but the visitor who has time is recommended to explore one of the residential quarters for himself.

Itinerary.

(The itinerary given here includes all the more important monuments and takes about three hours to complete. Time can be saved by those with less to spare by spending it only on monuments marked with an asterisk).

The ENTRANCE (1) to the excavations lies on the axis of the main thoroughfare of the earlier city which led from the Forum southeastwards, presumably towards a city gate. After crossing a street intersection and passing on the left a house with a small bathing pool the visitor reaches the narrow BYZANTINE GATE (2) which marks the southern limit of the city in the sixth century. Of the original structure, which like the flanking wall was built of re-used materials, the only surviving parts are the bottom courses of two rectangular towers (the east one perhaps used as a guard room) and a limestone threshold. At a later date a pier was added to the outside face of each tower to house a new or additional gate and a split cipollino column was used as a step to the higher level outside.

Continuing along the same street, which bounds an interesting residential quarter on the right the visitor comes to a TEMPLE (3) of unknown dedication on the left, standing (as do all but one of the Sabratha temples) in a colonnaded courtyard. The colonnades, composed of cipollino columns with Corinthian capitals of white marble, formed porticos round three sides of the courtyard, the temple itself being built against the western side. The western extremities of the lateral porticos are closed by semicircular apses, a feature of North African temple architecture which occurs again at Sabratha in the Temple of Hercules (15). Floors and walls of the apses and porticos are panelled in marble, but remains of stuccoed pilasters covered by the wall panelling show that the marble decoration is a later addition probably of the second century. An interesting and effective pavement formed of small rectangles of white marble laid in a herring-bone pattern surrounds the temple itself, of which only the lowest courses of the *podium* survive. There are traces of stucco on the sides, but marble steps on the front indicate that the decoration of the main elevation at all events was carried out in marble. Possibly marble and stucco were used simultaneously as in the case of the temple next to be described.

This lies on the opposite side of the street (where it expands to form a small piazza) and is known as the *ANTONINE TEMPLE (4) on the strength of an inscription (now placed at the top of the *podium* steps) mentioning the name of (?) M. Acilius Glabrio Cn. Cornelius Severus, an imperial legate for the Province of Africa in the reign of Antoninus Pius (A.D. 138-161). The temple and its surrounding courtyard *(Plate 12)* are shut off from the piazza by an elaborate marble-paved propylæum consisting of an entrance hall flanked symmetrically by a pair of smaller rooms accessible from the street only and a pair of larger rooms accessible from the temple courtyard only. Two cipollino columns with Corinthian capitals stood in each of the three inward-facing entrances. The general plan of the courtyard is very similar to that of the temple just described, except that the lateral porticos do not end in apses; the columns are again cipollino with Corinthian capitals and the floor is marble laid. The high *podium,* which is formally united with the thickened back wall of the courtyard by a continuous moulding, encloses two parallel and interconnecting crypts, to the first of which an entrance in the north side of the *podium* gives access. In front a flight of marble steps leads up to the porch which was formed of six Corinthian columns (four on the front and one for each return) carrying a marble entablature and pediment. The *cella* or temple chamber, which occupies the whole width of the *podium* and has a single door, is decorated externally with fluted pilasters, those in front being marble and responding to the porch columns, those on the sides and back of stucco. The interior of the *cella* has been disturbed by later habitation.

Returning to the piazza and passing a small late

fountain on the right the visitor enters the *FORUM (5) *(Plate 13)* through an entrance consisting of two white marble columns and a gateway. The north and south sides of the Forum are flanked by porticos of grey granite Corinthian columns. The portico on the east side has white marble columns and a coarse mosaic floor of a type which occurs again in the *atrium* of the fourth century Curia (11) and elsewhere. The north and south porticos probably mark the extension of the early imperial forum on these sides, though they are themselves later additions. But the east portico, which shows no signs of having replaced an earlier one, indicates a substantial reduction in the length of the original forum, in which the East Temple (6) and its surrounding courtyard seem to have been formerly included as an integral part of the general lay-out. If, as all the evidence suggests, the east portico was built in the late fourth century, this reduction is no doubt to be connected with the destruction caused by the Austurians in A.D. 365, after which the Christian population would not have restored a pagan temple and probably built the portico to shut off its ruins from the end of the Forum they used.

It is not known to whom the *EAST TEMPLE (6) was dedicated, but it seems to have been one of the most important of the city. It stands in a rectangular court-yard surrounded on three sides by slightly raised porticos, to which low continuous steps give access. Along the top of the steps ran a colonnade of stucco-covered sandstone Ionic columns with a row of Doric columns in the same materials behind. Of the temple itself the back and south side of the *podium* have survived and on the latter five of the stucco covered Corinthian columns which surrounded the *cella* have been restored, their height, for which there was no material evidence, being calculated according to Vitruvian proportions. Inside the *podium* may be seen traces of two earlier buildings: the first (on a different axis) apparently a house and perhaps of Phœnician origin; the other a temple with sides parallel to those of the later one but slightly smaller all round. Part of the *podium* of this earlier temple is still *in situ* immediately behind the south-east angle of the *podium* of the later temple. To support the front steps and porch of the new building two transverse foundations were added at the forum end, being largely constructed from materials taken from the earlier temple, including many bits of stuccoed moulding, some of them painted. The dating of the two temples is far from certain, but the later may perhaps be assigned to the second century and the earlier to the beginning of the imperial period or even before.

On the south side of the Forum lies the *BASILICA (7) which has undergone many transformations both as a pagan law-court (it was here perhaps the Apuleius of Madaura stood his trial for witchraft: see p. 43) and as a Christian church. The pagan Basilica consisted essentially of a long rectangular hall divided into nave and aisles by two rows of columns (of which only the footings survive) and terminating at either end in semi-circular apses, behind the western one of which lay a further chamber with a western door. Of this building the Christians used as the basis of their reconstruction the western apse (the floor of which was raised to form a presbytery), the chamber behind it (which became a baptistery, its external door being blocked) and the western two-thirds of the main hall, across which a wall was built to form the east end of the church. At the same time the north wall was rebuilt a little further to the south and the columns of the pagan Basilica were replaced by paired cipollino columns by which the span of the nave was reduced. This transformation is almost certainly contemporary with the general reconstruction of the Forum area at the end of the fourth century. Subsequently, most probably in the Byzantine period, various alterations in the internal arrangements of the church were made and the floor level was raised; but the main fabric was left untouched.

Immediately adjoining the north wall of the chamber behind the western apse is a building of square external and cruciform internal plan, which in its latest form was used as a BAPTISTERY (8). But two earlier periods can be distinguished in its interior arrangements. In the first of these the only entrance to the building was at the end of the eastern arm of the cross, the other arms being occupied by three low projecting platforms, the purpose of which is not clear. Floor, platforms, and walls were covered with marble panels. In the next period (probably late fourth century) the western platform was raised to form a canopied pedestal with an apse behind, while the others were suppressed by a general raising of the floor to their level, except in the centre where a narrow rectangular depression was left along the east-west axis, flanked on either side by three low and broad marble covered steps. In this form it closely resembled the Curia (11) and was probably used as a meeting-place by the authorities of the church with which it was now connected by a door in the southern arm. To make the Baptistery, which is a Byzantine alteration, the central depression was filled in with blocks of stone and a cruciform font of typical sixth century pattern was installed.

Next to the Baptistery and occupying the west side of the Forum stands the so-called *TEMPLE OF JOVE (No. 9), probably the main temple of the city. Its massive sandstone *podium*, which was covered in stucco, is prolonged in front to form an orators' platform, to which a pair of flanking staircases (the northern one is missing) gave access. From the level of this platform another flight of stairs extending the whole width of the *podium* led up to the temple porch which was formed of Corinthian columns carrying a pediment, remains of which can be seen on the platform. Pediment, columns and stairs were all of marble in their final state, but the existence of stone steps under the marble ones suggests that the original front elevation was treated in stucco. A row of columns ran along each side of the *cella*, but whether they were retained in stucco or changed to marble during the redecoration is not known. The *cella* has three thresholds indicating that the interior was divided into three chambers in conformity with the vaults beneath it. The vaults contain many fragments of inscriptions, friezes and other sculpture which fell into them when the temple was destroyed. Since the latest inscriptions date from the first half of the fourth century, the destruction was probably the work of the Austurians. The temple in its original state appears to have been built at the beginning of the imperial period. The redecoration in marble was no doubt done in the second century.

Behind the northwest corner of the Forum, with which it is not exactly aligned, stands the TEMPLE OF SERAPIS (10), identified as such on the strength of the discovery of a head of Serapis (an Egyptian god assimilated to Jove) during excavation. The temple is surrounded by a raised courtyard of the customary type, the north and south porticos having columns of grey breccia with Corinthian capitals. The rear portico, however, is formed of sandstone columns for a reason which is not entirely clear, but must be connected with some earlier version of the courtyard. Of the temple only the *podium* with a flight of marble steps survives. There are indications that the external walls of the *cella*, which occupied the full width of the *podium*, were decorated with stuccoed pilasters. The *cella* front had three entrances of which the thresholds survive; but the interior arrangements have been obliterated by later habitation. The corner of an interesting Byzantine house has encroached on the north portico.

The remaining side of the Forum is occupied by the fourth century *CURIA (11) in which the city magistrates met. It consists of a simple rectangular chamber opening on to a rectangular *atrium*, or colonnaded courtyard, to the east. The floor of the chamber rises towards the side and back walls in four broad, low steps on which the magistrates' seats were placed. The walls themselves are recessed to form a shelf supporting pilasters or, in the case of the more important back wall, detached columns. Floor and walls were covered with marble taken from earlier monuments; and part of an inscription so used has left its imprint in the cement undercoat of one of the steps. The *atrium* was surrounded by Corinthian columns (of cipollino along the sides and grey granite at the ends), each pair being joined by a stone arch. A small exhedra with an apse breaks the line of the northern wall in correspondence with an entrance in the southern wall. The paving is a coarse mosaic of large white marble cubes. An inscription carved on a reused base standing in front of the entrance to the chamber records

a dedication in honour of a certain L. Aemilius Q. fil...
for his « unremitting efforts on behalf of his needy
province and for bringing its plight to the emperor's
ears », an echo of the troubles of the fourth century.

Between the Curia and the sea stands the JUSTINIAN
BASILICA (12) *(Plate 14)* a building generally identified
with the « notable » church mentioned by Procopius as
having been built by Justinian at Sabratha. The main
body of the church, which is oriented, is rectangular
and divided according to the normal basilical plan into
nave and two aisles by two rows of columns. The
walls are entirely built of reused and badly fitting
masonry (mainly from the yellow limestone base of a
Severan monument near the theatre) and the columns
are a motley and incongruous collection from various
sources. Outside the west wall a roof carried on short-
ened cipollino columns formed a porch in front of the
three entrances at this end; there is believed to have
been an apse at the east end, of which, however, no
traces remain. Of the church's internal fittings there
survive *in situ* the pulpit (formed from a cornice block
from the Temple of Jove), the footing of the chancel
screen and the base of the altar with remains of its
supporting colonettes. The floor mosaic, the columns
which supported a canopy over the altar, and some
marble altar tables (the only features of the church
which can justify Procopius' description) have been
removed to the museum.

Opposite the east end of the Justinian Basilica is a
commercial quarter of the city containing buildings of
interest. Following round its seaward side the visitor
reaches a lane traversing the quarter from northwest
to southeast, at the north end of which, on the left hand
side, is a building containing a stone mill and cement-

lined basins, apparently the remains of an OLIVE OIL FACTORY (13). Turning left at the south end of the lane and taking the first turning to the right the visitor comes to the *SEAWARD BATHS (14), the largest of the Sabrathan bathing establishments, but still far from rivalling the Great Baths of Leptis. A marble-paved and marble-panelled room with an apse in the rear wall behind two cipollino columns forms an entrance hall from which on the north a door leads into a hexagonal latrine with marble seats and a deep flushing channel. The cipollino colonnade which supported the roof, the marble decoration of the walls and floor, the statue against the blank wall and the generous accommodation—it seated thirty—combine to give the room an appearance of monumentality and publicity curiously at variance with modern ideas and practices. To the south of the entrance hall a long passage with a black and white mosaic pavement (showing at least three periods of ancient patching) leads through two small rooms (one with two opposed lateral apses and the other rectangular) into a large room (perhaps the *tepidarium*) with a good coloured mosaic floor which has partly collapsed. Next to it on the north lies a room with a large rectangular bath, and beyond this a round-ended room with a raised floor for heating. The rest of the premises are too ruinous for their plan or purpose to be easily recognized.

Turning full left on leaving the entrance hall of the Seaward Baths the visitor reaches on the right a long street (containing many good examples of rain-water cisterns in the flanking houses) which leads through a modern aperture in the Byzantine walls into a transverse street linking the earlier part of the city with the theatre area. Shortly after a bend in this street which marks the junction of the two lay-outs (and after passing some Christian graves including an interesting late painted one) the TEMPLE OF HERCULES (15) is reached on the right. This is very similar in its general plan to the temple first visited (3). It stands against the back wall of a rectangular enclosure, the other three sides of which form porticos with cipollino columns and Corinthian capitals. Each lateral portico ends in an apse against the back wall. The porticos were paved with white marble, and a panelling of red breccia seems to have covered the lower part of the walls, including the walls of the apses where it has later been patched, partly with fragments of other coloured marble and partly with plaster painted in imitation of marble. The half domes of the apses and probably the upper part of the portico walls were painted with figure scenes. The only remains of the temple itself are the foundation courses. In front of it on a base stood a statue of Hercules, of which a fragment has survived. The temple was probably built when the surrounding area was developed in the second half of the second century.

Immediately east of the Temple of Hercules is a bathing establishment of rather confused plan, the original form of which underwent many later alterations. A large room occupying the southeast corner (probably the *tepidarium*) contains a bath on either side of a niche and its mosaic floor includes in its design two small medallions showing the various implements used in bathing. One of the medallions exhorts the bather to wash properly (*bene lava*), the other advises him that washing means health (*salvom lavisse*). North of this room lie various hot rooms with raised floors.

The second turning to the left to the east of the

bathing establishment leads down to two CHRISTIAN BASILICAS (16 and 17), both of which are of normal basilical form with raised west apses and two rows of columns dividing the body of the church into nave and aisles. The first and larger (16) incorporates part of an earlier building of which a mosaic pavement with the words *votum solvit* worked in it may be seen in front of the apse; and beneath this there are traces of a second pavement of concrete and mosaic belonging to a still earlier building. In its early period the church had a baptistery formed in two pre-existing rooms adjoining the south aisle; but at a later date a new baptistery was added on the north. Outside the east end is a colonnaded *atrium* or small courtyard in which part of the ruins of an earlier bathing establishment is incorporated. The smaller basilica (17) has two small chambers behind the apse separated from each other by a low wall. It was built over an earlier church from which these two chambers were lacking; and this in turn was built over the southeast corner of a much larger rectangular building of which the isolated column foundations and part of the walls have been excavated.

A little further along the shore to the east lie the OCEANUS BATHS (18), so-called from a mosaic head of the sea-god now in the museum. The *tepidarium*, where the mosaic lay, is symmetrically designed with an apse in the centre of its south wall and a bath to either side (with good mosaic decoration); but the warm rooms to the west follow no particular plan and are chiefly interesting for their clear illustration of an uncommon method of panelling walls for the circulation of heat.

About a hundred yards beyond the Oceanus Baths lies the TEMPLE OF ISIS (19), a building with many interesting features, but much damaged by cliff sub-sidence and erosion. It stood facing east in a rectangular enclosure decorated on the outside with pilasters. The east end of the enclosure (which lies on the other side of a stretch of fourth century city wall) formed an elaborate entrance with an external colonnade running along the top of a broad flight of steps and a second flight of steps leading down again on the inside. The courtyard was surrounded by porticos of stucco-covered sandstone columns with Corinthian capitals, and against the rear (west) wall stood a row of five adjoining chapels, presumably in connection with particular Isiac cults. The *cella* of the temple was surrounded by a colonnade on all four sides and stood on two parallel vaulted crypts, from the back of one of which a staircase led up to the back of the *cella* interior, presumably also for cult reasons. The arrangement of the front of the temple is not altogether clear, but the lower steps of the broad flight leading up to the porch can be seen.

To reach the Theatre directions are scarcely needed, since it is itself the most conspicuous landmark for many miles; but the approach from the Temple of Isis provides a convenient opportunity to visit the CHRISTIAN CEMETERY (20) to the northeast of it.

The *THEATRE (21) is justly the best known monument of Sabratha and also one of the most easily intelligible owing to the extensive but careful restoration carried out by the Italians. In its complete state the semicircular external wall of the auditorium *(Plate 15)* rose to the full height of the stage, there being a third row of alternate arches and pilasters above the two now standing. The sandstone exterior was covered in white stucco. Behind the arcades ran corridors, from the lowest of which six staircases led up to the higher rows of seats (not restored), and six radial passages gave access to an inner corridor concentric with the outer one. From the inner corridor five radial staircases led out into the middle rows of seats; while the lowest rows, in which distinguished spectators sat shut off by a semicircular screen terminating in two large carved dolphins, were reached by vaulted lateral passages between the auditorium and the stage. It is estimated that the theatre could hold about 5,000 spectators. Along the front of the stage runs a series of alternately rectangular and curved niches decorated with marble reliefs showing various mythological and theatrical scenes. The back wall of the stage or *scœnœ frons*, (probably the best of all surviving Roman theatres) is recessed to form three apses each containing an entrance and in front of it stands a continuous three-storied colonnade which follows the recession of the apses except where it projects to form rectangular porches in front of the entrances *(Plate 16)*. The storeys are of diminishing height and the top columns stand on pedestals. The capitals are composite (some of them decorated with masks and animal heads), and the columns are varied in material (those of travertine are modern) and in treatment, some being plain, some vertically fluted and some spirally. Above the stage a sloping ceiling was supported by beams projecting from the back wall. At either side of the stage are doorways leading to two large rectangular halls which must have been green rooms. The western one, slightly the larger, had an elaborate panelling of coloured marbles (part of which has been schematically reconstructed on the wall) and a series of compartments along the north side. Both rooms were marble paved. Behind the stage building lay a garden surrounded by a three-sided portico of sandstone Corinthian columns.

Immediately southwest of the theatre lies a curious PERISTYLE HOUSE (22), the peristyle or colonnaded garden being a feature of Hellenistic and Pompeian houses, but not occurring elsewhere at Sabratha. The colonnade, with one slightly curving end to its otherwise rectangular plan, is composed of rather squat fluted sandstone columns with Corinthian capitals carrying an architrave, part of which is preserved. Round the outside of the colonnade runs a sunken gallery leading to a series of underground rooms, one with remains of a mosaic floor. Gallery and rooms were originally covered with a roof resting on wooden beams of which the sockets are visible. There are interesting mosaics in some of the street-level rooms.

In the central room of the *MUSEUM (23) a plaster reproduction of the interior of the Justinian Basilica (12) has been made as a frame for its splendid mosaic pavement *(Plate 17)*. From an acanthus calyx at the west end of the mosaic (near the door as laid down in the museum) spring two intertwining vines with curving lateral branches laden with grape clusters. In this Vine of Paradise feed the souls of the blessed symbolized as birds. In some cases the symbolism is more specific: the phœnix above the calyx stands for the resurrection, the bird in a cage for the soul imprisoned in the body and the magnificent peacock near the pulpit for the glorified soul in heaven. On the side walls are the geometrically patterned aisle mosaics. Work of this quality is not found elsewhere in Byzantine Tripolitania and there can be little doubt that it was made by a craftsman brought from abroad; the pair of marble chancel screens on the end wall are certainly

7 bis

of foreign manufacture, screens of exactly the same pattern being found in Italy and elsewhere. In the other rooms of the museum are scultures, mosaics and paintings from the excavations, including the mosaic head of Oceanus already referred to on page 96 *(Plate 18)*. There is also an interesting collection of objects of everyday life (bronzes, ivories, pottery, glassware, etc.) found mainly in the residential and commercial quarters of the city.

Those who are interested in Roman bath constructions may like to finish this itinerary with a visit to the small SOUTHERN BATHS (24) which have a more clearly defined plan than the other baths of Sabratha. The entrance is marked by two columns to the right of a short flight of steps. Ahead through a small vestibule and a door lies a large rectangular room with two columns in the middle and a black and white mosaic floor considerably patched with later and coarser work. A door in the northwest corner leads into a small mosaic-floored latrine. The other rooms of the establishment extend to the east of the vestibule which has two columns on this side also. The first room (unheated) has a semicircular bath on the right and a hexagonal one on the left, both being decorated with mosaics; next come two round-ended rooms with hot pipes, and finally three hot rooms with raised floors. Beyond these rooms are remains of the furnaces.

Not included in this itinerary because of its distance from the other excavations is the second century AMPHITHEATRE (not on plan) which lies about half a mile to the east of the theatre. It appears to have been built in a disused quarry. A considerable part of the eliptical auditorium is preserved as well as several rows of seats. The general arrangements closely resemble those of a theatre. The arena, which measures about 65 metres by 49, is crossed by two sunken trenches and surrounded by a corridor with compartments for the beasts used in the spectacles.

iv. ISOLATED MONUMENTS AND REMAINS.

Although the main monuments of Roman and Byzantine civilization are concentrated in the three coastal cities, the Jebel and the wadis to the south of it (Soffegin, Zemzem and their tributaries) are rich in isolated remains, many of which are of great interest. But even if the material for a complete survey were available (which it is very far from being), it would be outside the scope of this little handbook to attempt it. For present purposes it will be sufficient to illustrate by a few examples the chief classes of monument likely to be found by those who have the good fortune to be able to visit more outlying places.

Olive Presses.

Olive presses (*torcularia*) may be seen in many parts of the country (including the garden of the Union Club in Tripoli), but they are most frequent in the area between Homs and el-Cussabat which has always been one of the most fertile parts of Tripolitania. They consisted originally of two vertical stone pillars, set close together with one or more stone crosspieces resting on their tops *(Plate 19)*. Between the pillars was hinged one end of a horizontal wooden lever under which the olives were placed in a pliable basket and crushed by pressure applied to the free end. The massiveness of the pillars and the addition of stones on top is due to the necessity of anchoring the hinge-end of the lever which would otherwise tend to rise during operation. The juice when extracted ran out of the basket on to a cemented floor and was collected in channels and troughs before being finally stored in large jars sunk in the ground. Good examples of *torcularia* may be seen at Breviglieri near Tarhuna (where the storage jars have survived *in situ*) and on the northern slope of Ras-el-Hammam near Leptis.

With the *torcularia* are often associated remains of other constructions connected with olive farming, including the proprietor's house. Next to the presses on the Ras-el-Hammam site lie the ruins of an elaborate country villa, the elegance of which is evident from the long colonnade with carved capitals which ran along its front. A little further down the hill are two well-built stone mausolea, the family tombs of the owners who seem to have been people of some wealth.

Constructions for the control of water.

Water has been one of Tripolitania's greatest problems throughout history. It is probable that in antiquity there was slightly more rainfall than now; for ancient field boundaries may be seen in places which to-day are nothing more than arid tracts of stone. Nevertheless the diminution has not been great enough to justify its description as a climate change. All the evidence of ancient writers, as well as the evidence of archæology, goes to show that the country has always lived close to the margin of drought in historic times. Somewhat paradoxically, when the rains do come, they come in too great quantities, concentrating their total annual fall into a relatively short period of the year. Since Tripolitania possesses a highly developed river system formed by the heavy rains of the Quaternary Age, these periodic floods are quickly drained from the land before use can be made of them, and often they do positive harm by carrying away great quantities of soil.

The methods adopted by the Romans to combat water scarcity and soil erosion are illustrated by remains to be seen in many of the wadis of the Jebel and further south. Wherever a catchment area presented itself, such as a roof or a convenient rock face, rain-water was collected and stored in cement-lined cisterns. Flood-water was controlled and collected by dams built across the wadis, some of them being constructed to break down the force of the torrent by imposing a partial barrier in its course, others being designed to block it completely and divert it into cisterns or irrigation channels. Examples of both partial and complete barriers may be seen in the Wadi ez-Zummit between Fonduk-en-Nagazza and Homs. Other barrages and walls, particularly those built across short and steep side wadis, seem to be more specifically intended for the prevention of soil erosion and for the formation of cultivation terraces.

Fortifications.

The establishment of a fully organized defensive system in Tripolitania was, as we have seen, mainly the work of Septimius Severus and his successors. The *Limes* proper, as given in a Roman itinerary of the early third century, began at Leptis and passed through stations called Mesphe, Thenedassa, Talalati, Vinaza, Auru, Thenteos, Thamascaltin and Thramusdusim before reaching the Tunisian frontier. Of these places none can be certainly identified. Only at Leptis itself are we on firm ground, since the first fortress of the series is almost certainly to be recognized in the ruins surmounting the hill of Ras-el-Hammam. The ruins appear to be those of a large rectangular building with an open central courtyard and rooms round the sides; but the original plan has been to some extent obscured by a Byzantine reconstruction in which only the north-eastern part of the Roman building was used. The two periods are clearly distinguished by different qualities of masonry, the Roman being more regular and very similar to other works of Severan date. Some cipollino columns and a fragment of a marble inscription (built into a mosque on the site) seem to suggest that some kind of temple was associated with the fortress, but it would have been an unusual combination. The rest of the *Limes* probably followed the southern slopes of the Jebel, enclosing the fertile areas of el-Cussabat, Tarhuna, Asabaa, Jefren and Giado; fortresses are said to exist in the Zintan area (near Ulad Duib between Jefren and Giado) and at Gash el-Berber (just south of Cabao on the Giado-Nalut road), of which the former has sometimes been identified with Thenteos of the itinerary, and the latter (on the strength of a local tribe called Slamatin) with Thamascaltin. But these identifications are far from proven.

It was an integral part of the Severan defensive scheme to strengthen the *Limes* by the construction of large isolated fortresses relatively deep in the interior of the country at the junction of important communications. Of these the best known surviving example is that of Bu Ngem on the eastern route from Leptis to the Fezzan. It was built, as inscriptions prove, in A.D. 201 under the supervision of the commander of the Legio III Augusta, Q. Anicius Faustus; and in accordance with the usual plan of a Roman *castrum* consisted of an open rectangular space (in this case measuring roughly 131 metres by 86) enclosed by massive masonry walls each containing a gate. Inside stood the various barracks, guard-rooms, offices, etc. Connected with the *castrum* was a little swimming bath in which was found the centurion's inscription already referred to above (p. 77). Two similar fortresses were situated in the Gheriat south of Mizda, commanding the central route to the Fezzan. The ruins of the first, at el-Gheria-el-Gharbia, include a triple-arched gate bearing the inscription, *pro(vincia) Afr(ica) Ill(ustris)*; while of the second, at el-Gheria-esc-Scherghia, three large walls are well preserved.

Fortified farms.

Some at least of the smaller isolated forts or fortified farms which occur so frequently along the wadis south of the Jebel (particularly Soffegin, Zemzem, Mimun, Scetaf, Nfed, Merdum and Busra) must date from the time of Alexander Severus when soldier-farmers were settled to cultivate and defend these outlying parts. But the only fortified farm which can be ascribed to the third century with any degree of confidence, is the Gasr el-Banata in the Wadi Nfed. This is a rectangular building with rounded external corners, measuring overall about 25 metres by 21 and standing to an average height of 6. The single door, which is set off-centre in one of the longer sides facing the wadi, has a simply moulded frame and is surmounted by an open arch above the lintel *(Plate 20)*. The interior has been reduced to a heap of rubble in which no plan is discernible, but remains of a moulded base, a spirally fluted column and an Ionic type capital show that it was to some extent decorated. The masonry throughout is of very high quality and much closer to typical Severan work than that of most of the other fortified farms.

Some of the most remarkable antiquities outside the coastal region of Tripolitania are situated at Ghirza, near the confluence of the wadi of that name and the Wadi Zemzem. They form three groups: two consisting entirely of mausolea to which reference is made in the next section, the other of some seventeen fortified farms and associated buildings situated on either bank of a small western tributary of the Wadi Ghirza, the Scia-et-Tmed. The buildings in the southern part of the settlement are grouped round an open rectangular space which has something of the appearance of a forum, while those in the northern part are laid out roughly in lines. Although, therefore, each building is fortified and capable of individual defence, they combine to give the impression of a small town. It has been suggested that the settlement is to be identified with Gerisa or Gereisa, a place mentioned by a Greek geographer of the second century after Christ; but it is difficult to reconcile this with the fact that all the visible remains are certainly late and there can be no question of the rocky ground concealing earlier foundations.

It will be sufficient to describe one typical building

of Ghirza since all the larger ones (and indeed most fortified farms elsewhere) follow the same general design: that of a rectangular courtyard surrounded by rooms built against the massive plain exterior walls. This is the plan (except for a slight angular bulge on one of the shorter sides) exhibited by the best preserved of the Ghirza buildings which stands at the southern extremity of the northern part of the settlement. It measures roughly 25 metres by 23 and is preserved to an average height of 7. The outside walls, built of small roughly squared stones, are of double thickness, the two skins being filled with stone rubble. The only external features are one or two small windows set high up in the walls and a few projecting perforated blocks for the tethering of animals. The single entrance is by a small door set off-centre in one of the longer sides and it leads through a narrow chamber presumably designed for defensive purposes. The rooms surrounding the courtyard were built to at least two storeys, possibly three, and remains of wooden floor-beams are still preserved in places. Wood was also used for the lintels of the internal doorways. Traces of a metal lined water pipe are another feature of some interest.

Ghirza is unique in giving the impression of a complete town in the desert, but the Wadi Soffegin, east of the point where it is crossed by the Mizda-Gheriat road, is rich in isolated buildings. One, in particular, the last on the left side of the wadi before reaching Nesma, is notable for the carved decoration of its doorway *(Plate 21)*. Judging from the remains of columns, capitals and other fragments of architectural sculpture lying about inside, the interior was no less elaborate; but apart from a well-constructed arch at the end of the entrance passage, the rest of the building is too ruinous for its internal arrangements to be recognizable. Simpler, but better preserved within, is a neighbouring building about a quarter of a mile to the west on the same side of the of the wadi *(Plate 22)*. It follows the general lay-out of the fortified farms of Ghirza, but differs from them (as do all the buildings in the Mizda area) in having vaulted instead of flat timbered ceilings.

Mausolea.

Mausolea, or funeral shrines, are found in many parts of the country, particularly along the top of the Jebel and in the cultivated wadis to the south, usually in association with a farm. The earlier examples tend to be square or nearly square structures, often of two or more stories, the lowest storey forming a sort of plain base or *podium* for the upper ones, which may be decorated with pilasters or open arches or sometimes with columns. In many cases a door at ground level gives access to a chamber with projecting brackets or recessed niches to hold portraits of the deceased, and there is frequently a burial crypt below ground. Good examples of this type of mausoleum may be seen at Leptis itself in the area to the northeast of the city an at Suk-el-Giumaa near Zliten, though in neither ca: is the upper part preserved. A large and elabora . mausoleum at Gasr Dugga (five miles northeast of Ta huna) with a more elongated plan and a recessed façad , had a third storey of Corinthian columns; and another at Henscir-es-Suffit (five miles southeast of Jefren) carries a small chamber with a projecting porch in the same position. Simpler tombs, consisting of a plain rectang-

nem. xvi.   Sabrata.   xvi. Ponto. xiii.   ass

xxvii.

Re.

ꝺ ᴄɪ ᴄ ᴇ ᴛ ᴠ ʟ ɪ.

ular *cella* with a small porch in front, occur at Tininaï in the Wadi Soffegin (between Bir-esc-Scedeua and Scemech) and at Germa (the ancient Garama) in the Fezzan.

Another form of mausoleum, composed of two stories of approximately square plan surmounted by a tall slender pyramid, is believed to have been introduced into Tripolitania from the Near East. The lower storey usually has pilasters or engaged columns at the angles and a decorated frieze and cornice on top. The second storey either repeats this scheme, or modifies it by replacing one of the walls by an arcaded opening, or consists entirely of columns carrying an entablature. A false door is often included in one of these storeys. The pyramid is plain, but in one instance at least was originally crowned by a Corinthian capital. Notable examples of pyramidal tombs exist in the Wadi Nfed (Gasr Umm-el-Ahmed), the Wadi Merdum (a pair 17 miles east of Beni Ulid. *(Plate 23);* and a single one another 20 miles east of these) and the Wadi Mesueggi (40 miles west of Beni Ulid). One of the best known of this type used to stand in the eastern necropolis of Ghirza where it was photographed intact in 1934, but it has since collapsed except for the lowest storey.

At Ghirza a third type of mausoleum is common. It consists of a rectangular *podium*, decorated with angle pilasters and an ornamental frieze, on top of which stands a solid *cella*-like core surrounded by four, eight or twelve columns supporting a continuous arcading *(Plate 24)*. In the larger ones a flight of steps leads up to the *cella* which is provided with a false door; and the whole structure has the appearance of a miniature temple.

The arcading and ornamental friezes of these mausolea *(Plate 25a)* have a decidedly « Byzantine » ap-

pearance; and a Near Eastern origin must also be sup-
posed for the heraldically opposed beasts which occur
on some of them *(Plate 25a)*. But the naive scenes of
everyday life (ploughing with camels and horses, reaping, hunting, etc.) and the « portraits » *(Plate 26a and b)*
are far removed from Byzantine art and can only be
the product of local carvers. Nor can the mausolea
have been directly connected with the Byzantines (for
instance with Belisarius' soldier-farmers), as has been
proposed, since there is nothing to suggest that they are
Christian monuments.

In the largest, and probably the earliest of the
Ghirza tombs *(Plate 27)* the form of a classical temple
is reproduced even more closely. It stands on a rectangular *podium*, of which the sides are prolonged at one
end to form flanking pedestals for a flight of steps, and
consists of a *cella* containing a chamber and surrounded
by a four-sided portico of « Ionic » columns supporting
a « Doric » entablature. There are no signs, however,
that there were ever any pediments. Remains of a very
similar mausoleum exist at Gasr el-Banat in the Wadi
Nfed, a short distance from the fortified farm already
mentioned (p. 104), with which the mausoleum was
clearly connected *(Plate 28)*. It has lost all its columns
and entablature, but the *podium* and *cella* are well
preserved. The *cella* contains a chamber and there is a
crypt beneath. The masonry throughout is of the same
high quality as that of the fortified farm and there can
be little doubt that the mausoleum is also to be dated in
the third century. The Ghirza mausoleum has every
appearance of being a later and more 'barbarized'
development of the same type.

Communications.

Although no remains of Roman roads, other than a few milestones, are known, there exist two documents from which something can be learnt of the system of communications in ancient Tripolitania. The first is the so-called *Tabula Peutingeriana*, or *Iter Pictum* (illustrated road map), an eleventh century copy of a Roman original of the time of Commodus (A.D. 180-192). The *Iter Pictum*, of which the Tripolitanian stretch is here reproduced (from a drawing), shows the communications of the empire in a continuous ribbon form, to conform to which the surrounding geography is schematically compressed. The other document is the *Itinerarium Antonini* of the early third century which lists the stations along the main provincial roads. The two documents are to some extent conflicting, but the most important line of communication, the coast road, is clear. From Tacape (Gabes) in Tunisia it followed the coast to Sabratha where it branched in two. One of the branches continued directly to Oea, while the other reached Oea after making a detour to the south and calling at a point marked by a large building in the *Iter Pictum*, probably to be identified with a place called Vax in the *Itinerarium Antonini*. At Oea the road divided again to meet once more at Leptis. The northern branch kept to the coast passing north of Ras-el-Mergheb in which area three milestones have been discovered, one dated in the reign of Claudius Tacitus (A.D. 276) and the others in the reign of Maximinus (A.D. 235-238). The latter stones record Maximinus' « constant care for the repair of bridges which have collapsed through age, and of roads ruined by long neglect ». The course of the southern road from

Oea to Leptis is uncertain. Halfway between Leptis and Tubactis Municipium (Misurata) the road again divides to make a small loop to the south joining again at the latter place, after which it follows the coast to Sirte and Cyrenaica with one or two unimportant side connections.

In addition to the coastal road the *Itinerarium Antonini* mentions a road « running along the *Limes Tripolitanus* from Tacape to Leptis Magna by way of Turris Tamelleni », the Tripolitanian stations of which have already been given in dealing with the *Limes* (p. 104).

For the caravan routes linking the coast with the Fezzan there is little direct evidence, but it can safely be assumed that they were the same as are used now. Geography allows little latitude for choice. Milestones have been found on the Tripoli-Garian-Mizda road *(Plate 29)* which was probably the main central route to the Gheriat, though another route seems to have passed through Beni Ulid and Ghirza. The main eastern route from Leptis must certainly have passed through Bu Ngem whence it probably touched Hun (Oasis of Giofra) before reaching the central Fezzan; while on the western route from Sabratha Sinauen and Gadames are the natural stages. Then, as now, there must have been many lateral connections between the main tracks.

Churches.

Finally brief mention must be made of three churches, which, though ruinous, are of considerable interest in themselves and throw some light on the question of the extension of Christianity in the interior of the country. The first is about two miles east of Breviglieri between Tarhuna and el-Cussabat and lies on top of a small hill just to the south of the road. It is of normal basilical type with a raised apse at the west end. There are two entrances, one at the east end of the north aisle and the other at the west end of the south aisle, to the latter of which a walled lateral approach was added at a later date apparently as a defensive measure. An unusual feature of the interior is the existence of a small single column in the middle of each side aisle. The main aisle columns had simply carved capitals, one of which may be seen on the ground. Many other fragments of the carved decoration of the interior are now in the garden of the Leptis Museum. A vestibule on each side of the apse leads through to the back rooms of the church which include a baptistery with a cruciform font. To the west of the church lies a fortified monastic house of which the original form has undergone considerable alteration by the addition of internal walls and staircases, perhaps connected with the building of a second storey.

The second church, also of normal basilical form, is situated at Asabaa about twelve miles southwest of Garian on the Jefren road. The east end is preceded by a rectangular ante-chamber, entered by a small door on the south and divided internally into three compartiments. Its purpose was probably defensive. Three doors in the west side of this chamber (which is also the east wall of the main body of the church) lead through into the nave and aisles which are divided by two rows of limestone columns with Ionic capitals. The footing of the chancel screen and the base of the altar may be seen in the western part of the nave. At the west end lies the raised apse, flanked on the north by a vestibule accessible from the interior and exterior of the church and containing a small staircase leading up to the apse from the back. Behind the west wall of the church are the remains of a baptistery with a four-lobed font.

The last church, which is the most southerly so far discovered in Tripolitania, stands on a projecting shoulder of high ground at the end of the short Sciaabet-Umm-el-Chrab (the first right-hand tributary of the Wadi Soffegin east of the Mizda-Gheriat road). It is known locally as the Gasr Chafagi Aamer. Its plain but sturdy construction *(Plate 30)* resembles that of the fortified farms of the neighbourhood, and it is comparatively well preserved except for the collapse of its vaults. Internally it is divided into nave and aisles by arcades carried on plain limestone columns and capitals. Since the vault of the nave was higher than those of the aisles, the difference was taken up by a clerestory wall above each arcade. The nave ends in a raised apse, the aisles in straight walls level with the front of the apse. Doorways in these walls lead into two low chambers which communicate with each other through a crypt under the apse floor. Along the back of the church, behind the apse and lateral chambers, runs a vaulted gallery. There are remains of a second storey above this gallery and the chambers; but it seems that it was in part at least a later addition. The whole of the interior of the church, including probably the columns and capitals of the arcades, was covered in stucco; and fragments of fresco decoration, in some of which the figures of saints are visible, still adhere to the walls. Behind the church is a baptistery and near it an oblong vaulted building divided internally into cells in which no doubt the priests lived.

GLOSSARY OF TECHNICAL TERMS

Apse
A semicircular recess in a wall, normally covered by a half dome.

Arcading
A continuous line of arches supported on columns.

Architrave
See Entablature.

Basilica
A rectangular hall divided longitudinally by rows of columns into nave and aisles. There is normally an apse at one or both ends. The name, which is believed to have originated in the Stoa Basileios at Athens, is applied to Roman law-courts and also to Christian churches which follow the same plan.

Cella
The internal chamber of a temple, usually rectangular.

Coffer
A decorative sunken panel on a ceiling or vault.

Conglomerate
Rough stone and rubble bonded with cement.

Corinthian
A capital sheathed in acanthus foliage and having four small spirals at the upper corners. There are many varieties in Roman architecture.

Cornice
See Entablature.

Doric
A capital shaped like a low bowl. Normally plain.

Entablature
The horizontal superstructure above the columns and below the roof of a colonnaded building. It is divided horizontally into three parts: the Architrave resting on the column capitals. the Frieze in the middle and the Cornice on top.

Exhedra	A recess or alcove in a wall, usually decoratively treated. An apse is a special case.
Fluting	The decoration of a column or pilaster with vertical or spiral furrows.
Frieze	See Entablature.
Ionic	A capital with a large volute or spiral roll at either side.
Janus	A four-sided arch, so-called from the Roman divinity of this name.
Mausoleum	A monumental tomb, often containing a chamber for the performance of funeral rites. So called from the colossal tomb of Mausolus of Halicarnassus.
Narthex	A porch in front of a church, to which in the early days of Christianity catacheumens were restricted before baptism.
Nymphaeum	A large fountain decorated with plants and statues.
Pilaster	A flat pillar attached to a wall for decorative or structural reasons.
Podium	The raised base on which the cella and columns of a temple or similar building stand. It usually has a moulding round the foot and a moulded cornice round the top, but is otherwise plain.
Portico	A roofed passage with a wall on one side and a row of columns on the other.
Propylaeum	A monumental entrance to a temple courtyard, usually ornamented with columns.
Spandrel	The triangular space between the curve of an arch, a horizontal line passing through its top and a vertical extension of its side.

ILLUSTRATIONS

PLATE 9.
Auditorium of Theatre,
Leptis Magna.

PLATE 11.
Arch of Marcus Aurelius, Tripoli,
from the East.

PLATE 14.
Justinian Basilica, Sabratha,
from the West.

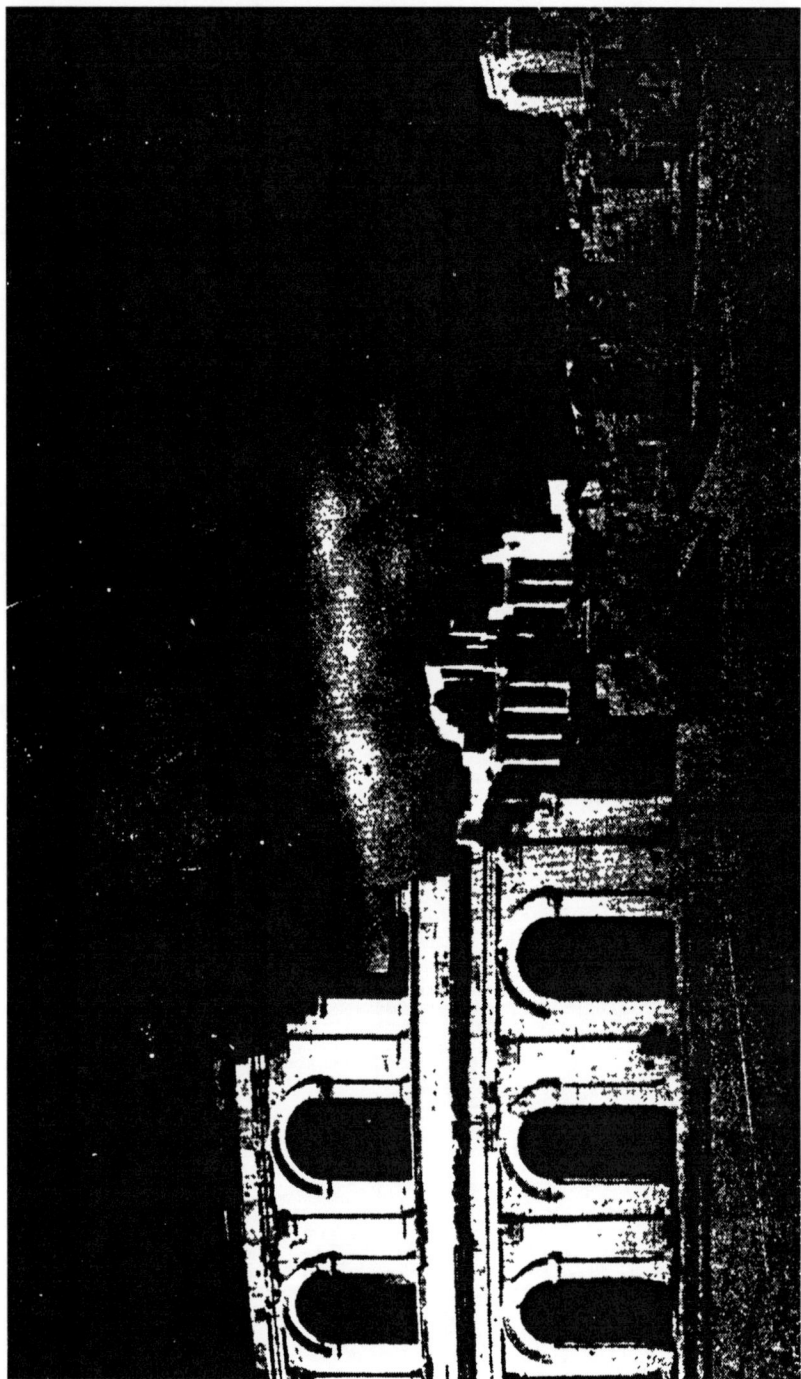

PLATE 17

Mosaic Pavement
of Justinian Basilica,
Sabratha

PLATE 22.

Fortified Farm
near Bir-en-Nesma,
Wadi Soffegin.

PLATE 25.

(a)   Detail of Mausoleum, Ghirza.

(b)   Relief from Mausoleum, Ghirza.

PLATE 27.
Mausoleum, Ghirza.

PLATE 28.
Mausoleum at Gasr el-Banat,
Wadi Nied.

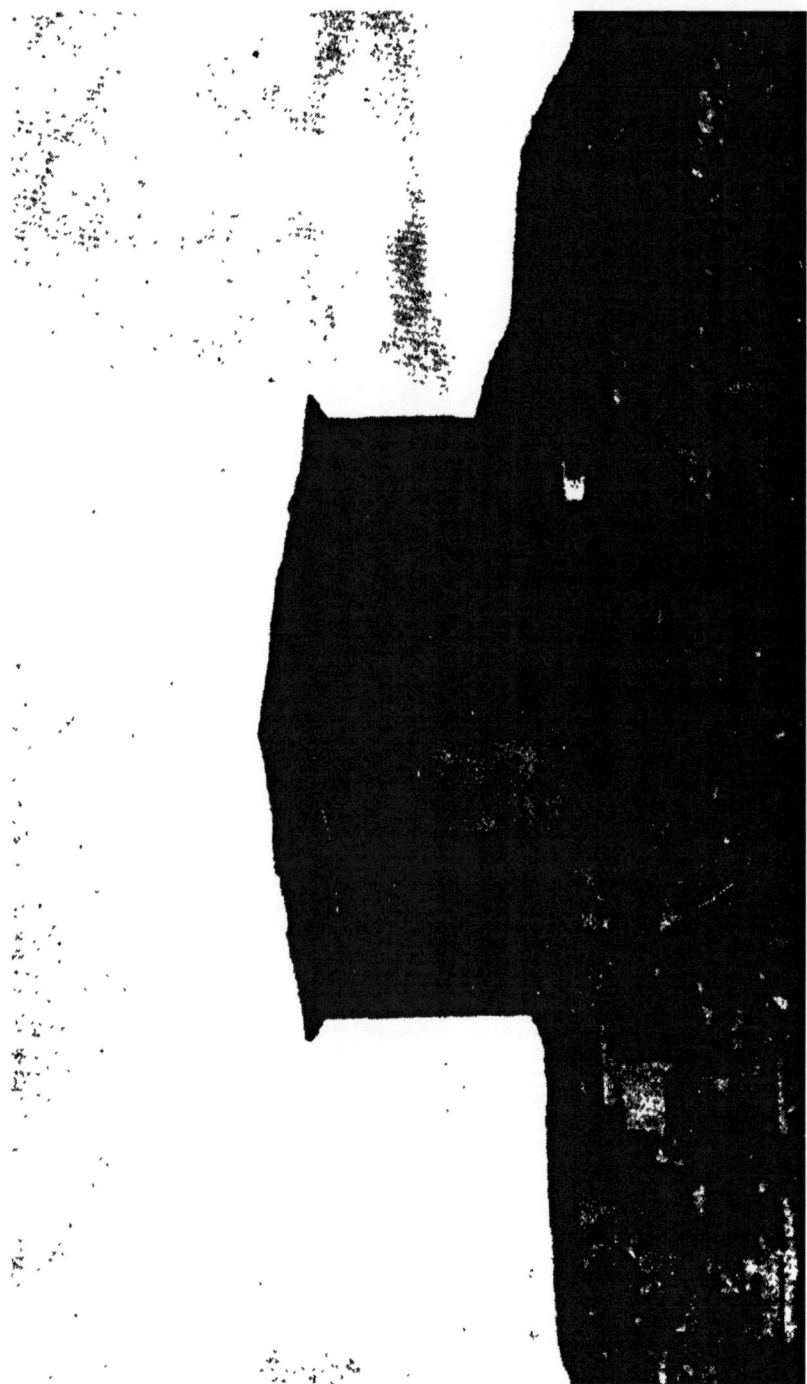

Lightning Source UK Ltd.
Milton Keynes UK
19 April 2010

153009UK00001B/257/A

9 781406 751857